Edmond About, W. Fraser (William Fraser) Rae

Handbook of Social Economy

The Worker's A.B.C

Edmond About, W. Fraser (William Fraser) Rae

Handbook of Social Economy
The Worker's A.B.C

ISBN/EAN: 9783744645171

Printed in Europe, USA, Canada, Australia, Japan

Cover: Foto ©Suzi / pixelio.de

More available books at **www.hansebooks.com**

HANDBOOK

OF

SOCIAL ECONOMY;

OR,

THE WORKER'S A B C.

BY

EDMOND ABOUT.

[*TRANSLATED FROM THE LAST FRENCH EDITION.*]

NEW YORK:

D. APPLETON AND COMPANY,

549 AND 551 BROADWAY.

1873.

CONTENTS.

INTRODUCTION.

A FEW years ago, M: Edmond About privately discussed, in a correspondence with Parisian workmen, several problems which personally interested them. They desired to ascertain whether, by associating together or otherwise, they could not materially better their condition. They avowed themselves ignorant of the doctrines of political economy generally current and accepted among educated and thinking men.

Two sets of opinions had invariably been presented for the acceptance of these working men; the one set giving them no hope of rising from a condition of comparative servitude to a state of independence, and inculcating contentment with their lot as an absolute duty; the other set being wholly revolutionary and subversive, upholding an appeal to force as the only sure means for at-

taining to comfort and opulence. Not being satis-,
. fied with remaining as they were, nor prepared to
have recourse to violence, they professed themselves
desirous of being instructed as to the real state of the
case, and ready to hear both sides. One. of their
number, who wrote on behalf of the others, asked M.
About: " Is there no science of Social Economy?
Why have we never been taught it? Are you versed
in it? Can you teach it to us? We do not ask for
a formal treatise, but a few hours of familiar talk
about Wealth, Capital, Income, Labour, Wages, Production, Consumption, Co-operation, Taxation, Money;
in fact, about the words which are dinned into our
ears, sometimes to dishearten, sometimes to dupe us,
but are never defined and freed from all uncertainty." M. About consented to undertake the
task. While engaged upon it, he thought that a
simple elementary work might prove useful to others
besides working men. " Whether agriculturists,
tradesmen, manufacturers, landlords, fund-holders,
artists, and men of letters, we all produce Social
Economy, as M. Jourdain made prose, without
knowing it. Unfortunately, we do not always make
it of good quality."

It appeared to M. About that, though elaborate
and valuable works abounded, there were few works
simply written and easily comprehended by every

reader, and that the result was prejudicial to the general diffusion of sound economic principles. Even the catechism of Jean-Baptiste Say, though a masterpiece of exposition, was addressed to a class of readers differing from that which now exists. A work which should prove acceptable to the more numerous reading public of the present day ought to be composed in a light and popular style. The necessity for such a work he states in the following sentences :— "No one is considered to be ignorant of the civil and penal laws which control us, and in reality no one is unacquainted with their broad outlines. Why should the large majority of such a nation as ours be still ignorant of economic laws, of these eternal and immutable laws which inevitably proceed from Nature herself? Why should the first innovator who comes to sap the foundations of society with paradoxes and sophisms take us always, or nearly always, unawares? Why are Capital and Labour, two allies bound together by Nature, eternally in opposition, not to say at war? Why do the worthiest men in the world reciprocally charge each other with dreadful crimes, the one crying that they are being stripped of what they possess, the others protesting that what they had not has been taken away from them? Why do the rich, or certain rich men, foolishly despise those who toil? Unhappy men, your fortune is nothing but consolidated labour. Why do the poor generally hate the rich? They do not know that they would be a hundred times poorer, that is, labouring more and earning less, if they were only surrounded by poor. Why should fraud and distrust, arrogance and revolt, absurd demands and unjust refusals, prevail in the domain of industry and commerce, where a good understanding would be so easy?" To these queries M. About replies that common ignorance of what is best alike for the individual and the community is the real source of mischief. His small volume will, he hopes, aid in dispelling this ignorance, just as the smallest light in a dark cave puts to flight the noxious creatures which revel and flourish in darkness.

The foregoing is M. About's own account, in an abridged form, of the origin and aim of the present work. His aptitude for writing it is beyond all question. He is largely endowed with the peculiarly French gift of rendering the most abstruse topics clear to the meanest understanding, and of making entertaining reading out of the driest and most unpromising materials. Among clever and cultivated Frenchmen he is pre-eminent for his skill as a popularizer of hard facts. One of his novels, *Maître Pierre*, is but an essay, in disguise, on the best way of reclaiming that uncultivated district in the South of France called the *Landes*. Another, the *Fellah*, is an exposition of the labour question in Egypt. Even *Madelon*, which has the appearance of being the mere picture of vicious life, is designed to uphold the advantages of co-operative agriculture. It is hardly an exaggeration to say that M. About could make Euclid as interesting as the most fascinating novel, and the multiplication table as amusing as a fairy tale.

He succeeds best where he has no personal views to propagate. His greatest failures have been his political opinions and previsions. So marked have been some of his blunders that there is danger of underrating his real powers. In this work there are some sentences and paragraphs which show that, when he wrote it, he was wholly unconscious of the inherent weakness of the deposed Imperial dynasty. Nor did he foresee, any more than many wiser men, that the year 1848 was not the end of the social revolt. He little thought, when penning the following, that a few years afterwards Paris would be under the rule of the Commune : " Socialism, which can be discussed to-day without heat, delivered its last stroke before our eyes in June, 1848. It is not only conquered, but is disarmed, owing to the progress of enlightenment and the better state of the public mind. Among those who toil and suffer in French society, a thousand men cannot be found who are so ignorant of their own interest as to seek alleviation in disorder and violence. The problem of universal well-being is not yet solved, I admit, but it is sensibly put, and that is a great point." (pp. 137, 138.) As a set-off may be quoted a remark which experience has amply confirmed :—" The members of the wages-class see or consider that they are on the eve of an economic movement comparable to the great rising of the volunteers in 1792, and each hopes that he has got his marshal's baton in his pocket." This rising took place without taking the exact form or direction which these men may have anticipated. It ended in the leaders, who had risen to high nominal rank, having either to save their lives by flight, or else to suffer life-long imprisonment or death.

One of the most notable and useful chapters in this work is the one on "Liberty." The character and effects of the Protective system are depicted forcibly and correctly. With the irony in which he is proficient, and the neatness of phrase in which he has no living superior, M. About sets forth how, under the pretext of increasing the wealth of French citizens and of advancing the greatness of France, successive governments kept the people in a state of tutelage, maintaining the passport system, prohibiting a baker to bake bread, a butcher to sell meat, a printer to exercise his calling, without permission from the authorities and without their constant supervision. The delusion of the Protective system is not, as M. About alleges, wholly due to the teaching or tyranny of monarchs. He has lived to learn that, in this matter, a Republic can be as short-sighted as a Monarchy. But at the time he wrote he might have witnessed the greatest and most genuine of modern Republics deliberately pursuing a course of policy as erroneous in an economic sense as any ever enunciated by the least far-seeing of European statesmen and enforced by the most ignorant of European kings. The following piece of argumentation applies to citizens in the United States as well as to French citizens:—"' Protect me!' says the agriculturist. 'I have had a good grain harvest; my neighbours, less fortunate, have barely doubled their seed. Before a month is over prices will rise, if the information in my newspaper be accurate. I hope to get thirty francs the hectolitre, and empty my granary under the best conditions in the world. I shall do this unless, through culpable weakness, the door is open to foreign grain! America threatens us, Egypt holds plenty suspended over our heads like the sword of Damocles; Odessa, infamous Odessa, thinks to glut us with her produce. Help!

Let the door be shut! Or, if you permit the importation of foreign grain, have the humanity to tax it
heavily, in order that the cost of purchasing on the
spot, the transport, and the import duty should raise
the price to thirty francs the hectolitre! If everything goes on as I should wish, I count upon pro-
ceeding to Switzerland, and bringing back four pairs
of oxen.'

" 'Protect me!' says the grazier. 'Shut the door
upon foreign cattle, if you wish me to earn a livelihood. We are promised a rise in the price of meat, and
I count upon it; but the admission of Italian, Swiss,
German, Belgian, and English cattle would create
plenty for everybody and be my ruin. Protect
me by prohibiting or by taxing all the products
which come into competition with me. Let grain
enter; I do not grow any, and I like to buy bread
cheaply. Permit the entry, free of duty, of the combustibles with which I warm myself, the glass out of
which I drink, the furniture which I use, the stuffs
with which I clothe myself, and all manufactured
products in general. Oh, visible providence of citizens,
arrange so that I shall not have any competition to
fear as producer, but that in what I consume I may
enjoy all the benefits of competition.'

" 'Protect me!' says the manufacturer. 'Cause all
the products which compete with mine to be seized at

the frontier; or, if you suffer them to enter, load them
with a duty which will render them unsaleable. The
interest of the country enjoins upon you to serve my
personal interest. Do you not take pity upon the
national industry doubly menaced by superior qualities and lower prices? My foreign comrades may
reduce me to destitution by inundating France with
good merchandise at cheap rates. As a citizen I fear
no one in Europe; as a manufacturer I am afraid of
everybody. The feeblest foreigner is stronger than
I. Strive then that I may preserve the monopoly of
my products; but be generous as regards all that
which I buy but do not sell. Allow grain to enter,
in order that my workmen, being fed for next to
nothing, may be satisfied with low wages. Allow
the raw materials I employ to enter, and the machines
which assist my labour.'

" 'Do nothing of the kind,' exclaims the machine-
maker. 'If the foreigner should come and compete
with me, there will be nothing for it but to shut up
shop. Stop, or tax, the products which resemble mine;
content yourself with opening the door to the metals
I use, and you will usefully protect the national industry as far as I am concerned."

" 'Hold, there!' replies the iron-master. 'If
foreign iron be admitted, I must put out my furnaces.
Leave me the monopoly of my industry; only allow

me to import freely the minerals and combustibles which are my instruments of labour.'

" ' No, a hundred times no ! ' reply the shareholders in mines and coalpits, and the proprietors of forests. ' Is our industry less worthy of protection than the others? Now we shall be ruined if foreigners are permitted to introduce plenty and low prices amongst us.'

"Deafened by such a concert, it is not surprising that statesmen should have been induced to tax all imported articles, or nearly all." (pp. 148—151.)

Instead of entering upon a minute criticism of the economic doctrines propounded by M. About, I may state generally that they are sound in the main, and are borrowed from the leading authorities. Sometimes he pushes the views of these authorities beyond a point at which the principal English and French economists have stopped short. For example, it is not customary to rank medical men among producers. Yet M. About does so, and on grounds which are very plausible, if not scientifically accurate. The reasoning in this case is similar to that employed in others of an analogous kind. The passage itself is a good illustration of M. About's characteristic ingenuity: "Do you grant that among the things useful to man, the most useful is man himself? Do you accept the calculations of the economists who

say that, commencing at his twenty-seventh year,
the individual reimburses the advances made by
society? Do you think, like J. B. Say and all who
reason, that the problem is not how to beget children,
but how to rear them to man's estate?.

"You ought then to acknowledge that the medical
art, by organizing a struggle against the destructive
causes which threaten us from our birth, produces an
incalculable amount of utility on earth. Our life,
according to Bichat's definition, is the aggregate of
the forces contending in us against death. Every
hour, Nature claims the elements of which our body is
composed; our existence is but a militant loan, incessantly continued and renewed: it would be impossible to rate too highly the fine medical industry
which protects the human being against a universal
conspiring host.

"Among the men of your acquaintance, are there
many whom science has not once rescued from death?
Starting from that point, say whether the doctor of
medicine is a more paltry producer than the cabinet-
maker or the stone-cutter?

"Jean Jacques Rousseau, and all those who have
made mouths water in celebrating the state of Nature, are detestable jesters. For man, the state of
Nature is a state of filth, of privation, of innumerable maladies, and premature death. We still know

a certain number of tribes who live in a state of Nature. In their case the average duration of life, in the most genial climates, is from twelve to thirteen years. Among the civilized nations of Europe, thirty years is the average. Without leaving our own country, we can recognize a sensible difference between the life and health of a badly cared for peasant and of the citizen who dwells close to Dr Robin and Dr Nelaton.

"Having said that, I incline to think you will not decline to inscribe the Doctor in the first rank on the list of producers." (pp. 38, 39.)

To many persons the purely social side of this work will be its strongest recommendation. While enunciating the leading truths of economic science, M. About loses no opportunity of giving them a personal application. His special aim is to bridge over, if possible, the gulf which separates the rich and the poor, or rather, to demonstrate that the gulf is more of a figment than a fact. He insists upon the interdependence of mankind, and denies that progress is possible unless the poor help the rich, and the rich benefit the poor. In proof of this the following passage may be cited :—"As for you, rich men, you would do the most foolish thing in the world, if you should dream of perpetuating the poverty and ignorance of others. Are you unaware that poverty and ignorance condemn the healthiest and most robust individual to a sort of quasi-sterility ? That the more one knows, the more one is able to produce ? That good intentions being equal, an educated working man renders ten times more services than an ignorant one ? That tools, namely, the beginning of riches, often increase the quantity of useful labour tenfold and a hundredfold ? That actual, contemporary labour, with which you cannot dispense, will cost you so much the less the more it is offered, will be the more offered the more easy it is, and will be all the easier the better it is enlightened or equipped ? I add, merely that it may be borne in mind, a consideration which has its value, namely, that the security of your persons and property will constantly increase in proportion to the degree of public wellbeing and education.   Will you now deny that self-interest, rightly understood, impels you to instruct and enrich those who are destitute ?

" Hence the poor man ought to wish for the opulence of the rich, and do so in his own interest.

" The rich ought to wish the poor to be well off, and do so out of pure selfishness.

"And social economy ascends to such a height that it merges into universal morality.   For man's reason is indivisible, and there are no truths which cannot be reconciled with each other.   What would happen if

the poor, out of calculation, were to apply themselves
to enrich the rich ? If the rich, out of a wise selfishness, were to apply themselves to enrich the poor?
Who would be the gainer in such an event ? Everybody.

"The area we inhabit is limited, but the production
of useful things is unlimited. Oh ! how fine would
be the victories and how vast the conquests if, instead of fighting against each other, we were to
unite all our efforts against blind and stupid nothingness! " (pp. 122, 123.)

It would be easy to go through the several
chapters, pointing out noteworthy remarks and extracting interesting passages. Enough, however, has
been said to show the character of this work, and to
induce those whose curiosity has been excited to read
it and judge for themselves. Many things in it are
instructive as exhibiting the course pursued in
France relative to economic problems, some of which
have been dealt with and settled, others being still
among the puzzles of the hour. The work itself is
a new and most readable sermon on the text, " In
the sweat of thy face shalt thou eat bread." The
conclusion arrived at may be expressed in the words
of the Koran: " Man hath nothing to expect save
from the fruit of his labour."

W. F. RAE.

HANDBOOK OF SOCIAL ECONOMY.

CHAPTER I.

MAN'S WANTS.

LIFE would have been a sad gift to us had we received nothing besides.

The new-born man is undoubtedly the most forlorn and feeble, and, for the longest time, helpless, of all the animals which multiply on the earth.

To abandon a little child in a lonely place, or to break its head against a tree, is the same thing. Nature has so formed us that, in order to exist, we require shelter, clothes, food, and a thousand things which she does not provide, and with which we cannot supply ourselves.

During several years our fellows lodge, clothe, and feed us; society gives us credit. We live but as debtors till the age when we can more or less adequately shift for ourselves. A time comes when a young man nearly earns his keep, and lives with a comrade, after the fashion of shopmen and apprentices. At length, towards our twenty-seventh year, if the economists are to be credited, we begin to earn more than our cost, and to repay the advances made to us by society.

Children — and I know many men who are children in this respect—suppose that society owes them something. Have you never heard the famous maxim—" To each one according to his needs " ?

As for me, I thought it admirable in 1848. I was then twenty years old, and, to put it concisely, was as ignorant of life as a good school-boy. I had done nothing but themes and exercises, which are certainly of no use to the community, and I innocently considered myself a creditor. I did not understand that a youth like myself, having a good appetite, was disentitled to claim his share in the delicious products of the earth. Was not the earth itself in some sort my patrimony? It seemed to me the height of injustice that, out of the billion of human beings spread over a given surface, another should have confiscated and cultivated the slice which pertained to me ; because, forsooth, had not I the right to live ? Therefore, I had a natural and acquired right to all the necessaries of life.

Spare your scoffing if I admit that it took several

years to disabuse me of my illusions concerning the true notion of right.

Man is a divine creature, because he is the final product of the creation, because Nature has formed nothing more intelligent and more capable of improvement than he. Each of us enters at birth into the heritage of a sovereignty which renders his person inviolable. In principle, if not in fact, we are all equal, because we all share the same august character. We are all free-born in this sense, that no one has a title to subject another to his will by force. Right signifies neither more nor less than the inviolability of the human species.

If the planet we inhabit were a terrestrial paradise, granted to all who are or may be born in order that they may enjoy themselves without toil, the deed of gift would confer on all of us an equal right to everything which is necessary, useful, or agreeable. We should share among ourselves the enjoyment of the common inheritance, whilst making a few sacrifices in favour of our successors. Press the hypothesis of a terrestrial paradise to its conclusion, and you will see the human race living on the earth like flies in a dining-room. Generations continuously succeed each other throughout a series of years without these fortunate insects having perfected anything around or belonging to them.

What constitutes the greatness and glory of our species is the difficulty of living where we are cast. At our birth we are dowered with needs more complex than those of all other animals whatever, and the earth obstinately withholds that which would satisfy them. The earth yields nothing save to labour; if we desire shelter, clothing, and food, we must forcibly obtain them, and extract them from the earth's bosom. Everything which is of use to man is the prize of man's exertions.

Now, labour is the exercise of our faculties, and practice makes perfect. Hence the necessity of improving the state of things inevitably existing around us leads to our own improvement.

In proportion as man becomes perfect new needs arise, and these give birth to new efforts, and thereby he is constantly made to surpass himself; such is the history of the progress of humanity.

Much has been said, during the past two or three years, about a fine fellow living as a savage in the forests of the Var. As a monomaniac he is interesting, and his endeavours to diminish his wants merit the attention they have received. But this worthy semi-idiot takes civilization against the grain. To consume little without producing anything is not to rise above humanity, but to sink to the level of beasts. This poor wretch may indeed confine himself to what is strictly necessary; he robs us, for he will die insolvent, and will in no wise repay society the sacrifices it has made for him.

It is excellently said by Say that the most civilized man is he who produces and who consumes the most. Compare the Hindoo sluggard, who works a quarter of an hour in order to procure a handful of rice, and who lives upon this for a whole day, with the English workman, who consumes butcher's meat, vegetables, beer, cloth, gas, coal, and metallic substances, and produces in proportion. Which of the two makes the larger addition to the capital of the human race?

If you wish to form a notion of the requirements which civilization has engendered, and the resources it has placed at your disposal, suppose all these resources to fail you simultaneously, and that, with all your wants, you were cast upon a desert island.

Imagine a man of thirty-five years of age, in the fulness of his strength, robust, trained, clever, and educated; indeed, whatever you please, yet alone and forlorn on a shore whereon no other man had set foot. How many days would you give him to live?

Two centuries ago this problem was stated in very different terms, and in such a way as to simplify its solution, by the illustrious English novelist, Daniel Defoe. The island on which Robinson Crusoe is cast

2

appears to be formed expressly for him; ferocious beasts are not introduced, and the climate is ameliorated beforehand. His ship, which he strips at his leisure, furnishes him with provisions, clothing, shoes, tools, arms, munition, and even domestic animals. These constitute the materials of European civilization; they are a superabundant capital, the accumulated labour of more than sixty centuries placed within the reach of a single shipwrecked mariner. This pseudo-pauper has even luxuries, books, money, and what not. By the accident which cuts him off from society, he becomes the casual heir of one hundred millions of persons. Still, you must allow that you are disquieted about him. You cannot consider the matter without saying to yourself that the wants of a civilized man are far more numerous, more complex, and varied than the cargo of any ship whatever can supply.

What if the man were really left to his own resources? What if the ship were absent?

Imagine as rich an isle as you can, one with ten metres of vegetable mould spread over the surface of the soil, and all the trees that earth spontaneously yields. Fish swarm in the waters, the air is peopled with birds, every description of game abounds in the woods. But neither game nor fish court death; arms, nets, instruments are required to capture them. Moreover, the natural products of the soil are usually insipid, and sometimes poisonous. Besides, man cannot live on raw food, and there is no fire. Fire! that is a trifle for the Parisian who has lucifer matches in his pocket, and who meets lighted cigars all along the street. Yet merely lose your way in the wood of Vincennes, be overtaken by night, suffer cold, and try to make fire as the savages do by rubbing two pieces of wood together. Exhaustion will come more quickly than a spark.

The construction of the rudest shelter, were it but a simple hut formed of intertwined branches, implies an axe, a knife, an implement of iron or stone keen enough to split wood. Alas! the first piece of iron seems far to seek when we picture ourselves in a state of Nature. How many generations have toiled to attain this goal! In Paris we can purchase a knife for a sou, a box of matches for a sou, and a roll of bread for a sou, and we forget that the first discoverer of fire, the first sower of corn, the first blacksmith, were ranked as gods.

Clothing is so common among civilized persons, we are so much accustomed to see those around us clad, that it almost requires an effort of imagination to picture a body stark naked. Take a schoolboy and ask him to draw a man; he will begin with the hat. To us, perfect nakedness is represented by tattered garments, worn-out shoes, a dirty and bat-

tered hat; we do not figure to ourselves the human
body exposed directly, without any defence, to the
inclemencies of heat and cold, to the wind and the
rain, to the rugged and stony ground. Civilized
man, whether he be rich or poor, does not strip off
his clothes save when he takes a bath or goes to bed.
The bed itself is a covering, softer, pleasanter, and
more comfortable than the others. All the French
do not possess spring mattresses and linen sheets, yet
it is possible to number those who have not a bed of
some sort in which to lay themselves down at night.
When we wish to convey the notion of a wretched
bed we speak of a hard and filthy truckle-bed, without dreaming that this truckle-bed would be the ideal
of comfort to the naked beings who sleep on the bare
ground.

What conclusion follows from this? It is that the
simplest and the most primitive form of existence is
exceedingly complex. The merest trifle, that which
costs next to nothing because it superabounds in a
civilized land, is the product of incalculable efforts.
The shipwrecked sailor of whom we have just spoken,
would wear his fingers to the bone before he could
quarry and prepare one of the paving-stones on which
you walk, exclaiming—" Oh, how wretchedly this
street is paved ! "

I shall suppose the shipwrecked sailor, at the

close of the first day of exploration and toil, exhausted, his hunger imperfectly satisfied with fruit and wild roots, reclining under the branches he has broken off, on a bed of dried, pointed, and penetrating grasses, which he has torn up one by one. He goes to sleep, if indeed a civilized man can enjoy true slumber amidst innumerable dangers. Security is a benefit upon which you lay no store because it is so common. However, he falls asleep, and dreams this dream :—

Two young and healthy beings are reposing in a wooden bed furnished with mattresses and a coverlet, not to speak of two pillows and two linen sheets, in a small and well-closed chamber. An infant sleeps in its cradle alongside of them. This family is protected from intrusion, first by an excellent wrought-iron lock, then by a porter living at the foot of the staircase, lastly by a policeman, who traverses the street from night to morning. No rain, wind, noxious animals, nor savage creatures can enter this humble yet happy dwelling. All the necessaries of existence are to be found there, if not in abundance, still in sufficient quantity, for the remains of a meal are on the polished walnut table—a lump of bread, a piece of beef or veal on a plate, a portion of the vegetables in season, a jug half-filled with fresh and clear water, and wine, that support and solace of man, at the bottom of a bottle. Four straw-coloured and varnished wooden chairs, a night-table, and a walnut chest of drawers with marble top, complete the furniture of the room. The drawers, which are fastened with locks, contain a heap of things for which the shipwrecked sailor would give many years of his life; light and warm woollen garments, a small supply of bleached and well-sewn linen, needles and thread, buttons and pins, forming a real treasure for a man who has retained all the needs of civilization, while losing at one swoop all its benefits. Superfluities are added to necessaries; a candle, matches, a book, a silver watch, are on the night-table. The walls are hung with paper, and ornamented with four framed prints. Some very modest luxuries, in truth, yet such as a castaway could not produce after labouring for ten years, adorn the black marble chimney-piece.

Were the shipwrecked sailor an ex-millionnaire, he could not help feeling envious at this sight. These persons, then, are earthly sovereigns? They have laid the universe under contribution in order to lodge, nourish, and clothe themselves?

An architect has traced the plan of the dwelling they inhabit, a quarryman has disembowelled the earth in order to procure the stones; a tile-maker has extracted, dried, moulded, and baked each of the tiles which shelter them; a woodman has felled trees in the forest, which a waggoner has transported, they have been squared and arranged by a carpenter so as to form a roof for them. A plasterer has prepared the lime which covers their four walls. A joiner has planed their floor, their door, and their window. A painter has coated the woodwork with several layers of colour prepared by a chemist. A glass-blower has moulded their window-panes, which a glazier has cut with a diamond brought from Brazil by a crew of sailors. What a number of miracles wrought on behalf of a single household! How many people have traversed the seas for the profit of these persons! The coffee, whereof there are dregs at the bottom of their cups, comes from Java, their sugar from the Antilles, their pepper from the Spice Islands, the small clove which flavours the soup has been taxed by the Iman of Muscat, on the east coast of Arabia. The stock-breeder, the butcher, the labourer, the miller, the baker, the vine-dresser, the salt-maker, the oil-man, the vinegar-maker, the weaver, the spinner, the dyer, the mercer, the blacksmith, the tailor, and a hundred other members of the community, have worked for these three persons. Had I ten thousand slaves at my command they would not procure for me one-half of the useful things which abound in this garret. I should have to work twenty-four hours daily during ten years in order to fabricate a single nail in these shoes, and should fail in the endeavour.

Intelligent reader, these happy ones of the earth who have bread upon their table and nails in their shoes, need no introduction to you from me. You have recognized them, and who knows if you have not recognized yourself in them. They form a small household of Parisian workpeople. The husband earns five francs, and the wife one franc fifty centimes, a-day.

Yet the master of this lowly dwelling is unaware that he is envied by the shipwrecked sailor, and by many besides; for instance, by the Russian porter who sleeps in a barrel before his master's palace, or the poor Roman reaper who swallows dust and sweats like a dog from the rising of the sun unto its going down. He would be greatly surprised were he told that he is better lodged, better fed, better clad, and vastly more civilized than certain knights of the Middle Ages, and even than all the kings of the Iliad and the Odyssey.

He too dreams, but of what? About the dangers from which he is free? No. About the privations from which mankind suffered formerly, to which semi-barbarous tribes are now exposed? No. He dreams about the affluence of his master, an important manufacturer, who has built a mansion on the

Boulevard Haussmann, and has just purchased a country seat.

Is not his master happy? In the course of two hours he does his day's work, whilst the workman must labour for ten hours. He goes and comes, drives whither he pleases—in the park, to the races, to the opera. Should the fancy strike him, he takes the express train, and sees a hundred leagues of country in a few hours. He has an elegant wife, with white hands; he bestows upon her all that is costliest in the world. He has masterpieces of painting in his room, a library filled with the rarest editions of the best works.

" As for me, I read as much as I can ; yet what is to be done when one is occupied ten hours daily ? I cannot choose my reading ; I must select whatever is cheapest ; and it is notorious what horrid trash cheap literature is. Five or six times a year I go to the theatre ; but the workman cannot make choice of the plays he sees. Instinctively I delight in what is striking and splendid, but my position does not permit of my liking being gratified. What avails it to visit a museum on a Sunday, when the crowd is dense, and there is neither explanation nor commentary ? What are the concerts organized among ourselves, between friends, in our choral societies ? What is the dusty and plastered Nature

of the suburbs, which alone we behold in the spring?
I love my little wife, and am grieved to see her
reduced to work like me. Something tells me that
the master of a household should be able by himself to provide for the wants of his family. Thus it
is in the case of my master and of rich people: when
will it be thus in our case? It vexes me also to see
my wife wretchedly dressed; I am annoyed not to
be able to give her more than the fag-end of each
day of toil, the scraps of my life, the fragments of
my time; my heart tells me that one loves far
otherwise and far better when one is not enslaved by
the requirements of existence. I idolize my little
boy, and my blood boils at the thought that, barring
a miracle, he will be a workman like myself. I
shall send him to the grammar school, but the
higher schools are as inaccessible to him as the
Lord's Prayer is to donkeys. Cannot a scheme be
devised to change all this? What is the use of
inventors? Where is progress? I would even
resign myself to struggle all my life, if I had but
the hope of leaving this little fellow less of a day-
labourer than we are."

But do you think that the master, who is no
day-labourer—the master who does not receive
wages, but pays them—the great manufacturer, the
man rolling in luxury, is in want of nothing? He

has enough wherewith to satisfy the ambition of a hundred Parisian workmen, to save the lives of ten thousand shipwrecked sailors dying from cold and hunger; yet his wants have altered with his condition.

You imagine, perhaps, that he awakes in the night to congratulate himself upon his possessions? Not so : if he awake, it is rather to think about the good things he lacks.

Man is so constituted that, stage after stage, he regards as a fresh starting-point the place which he has reached.

We take the advantages for granted which we have gained by chance or exertion, and we hasten to think about others.

The head of a manufactory is no more sensible of the pleasure of riding in a carriage, than you or I of the pleasure of wearing shoes.

Assuredly, he is not to be pitied whose day's work is done in two hours. Yet in the long run these two hours of daily labour become fatiguing to him, the more so because business anxieties occupy him during the intervals. He is harassed by the uncertainty which is the lot of fortunes invested in industrial pursuits; he longs for the moment when he can render himself safe by exchanging this complicated, absorbing, and exhausting method of work for another much simpler, equally potent, and self-acting.

The desire is accomplished : the manufacturer has become a fund-holder. Out of every twenty-four hours of the day he can henceforth claim twenty-four as wholly his own. You suppose that all his wants are satisfied; yes, all his former wants are satisfied, but others immediately arise. This happy man perceives the contrast between the amount of his fortune and the extent of his education, and he is sorrowful. On leaving business, he has entered a society wherein nearly every man is better trained, more refined, more polished than he. Among those who are emancipated from personal struggles for existence, merit determines precedence. That he possesses merit is proved by his having made his fortune; but no sooner is this done than the rich man is called upon to show merit of another kind.

Since he has had leisure to look over his library, he has daily found his mind lacking in many things. Since frequenting the rooms where conversation is carried on, he has observed that the persons with whom he associates know more and converse better than himself. Since he has been able to spend every summer in the country, he has learned that the country is an unknown world to him. Since he has been in a position to take part in public life, as others do, he has found that much must be acquired if he would escape ridicule. In short, this rich man has become poorer than ever, because the material wants which no longer disquiet him, are succeeded by a legion of mental and moral wants as imperious and despotic as the former, and far less easily satisfied. For him, too, there are hours of discouragement, and more than once he exclaims, as he casts his book aside, "Oh that I were certain my son would be less idiotic than myself!"

The endless series of our wants growing the one out of the other with constantly increasing vigour, compels us ever to move on from point to point towards a goal which humanity can never reach. For on the day when there is nothing to be perfected in or around us, we shall have ceased to be men, and shall have become gods.

We must admit, without being cast down, that the earthly pilgrimage is a journey after the unattainable, in which there is neither halting nor repose. Yet, as we proceed, we see springing up under our feet that mass of useful arts which constitutes humanity's patrimony.

CHAPTER II.

Utility does not require to be defined. Nevertheless, an explanation of it may be profitable.

Many years have elapsed since man appeared on the earth. Geologists affirm that, before our appearance, this little globe moved round the sun for thousands and thousands of ages. During that period the soil, the sea, and the air were of no benefit to anybody, because no one existed here below. A multitude of plants and animals was created before the germs of the first men were formed: these plants and animals, whatever properties and powers they might have had, were entirely useless, because utility, as we understand it, means the service which a thing might render to man; therefore, there was nothing useful prior to man's advent in the world.

Man is born, and all beings at once take rank in

relation to him. The wild beast, rushing to devour him, enters into the first category of noxious things; the poisonous plant reveals to him its baneful properties; the thorns which prick his limbs, the insects which prey on his body, are noxious to him in degrees varying according to the amount of pain which he suffers or dreads.

The timid animals that flee before him, the plant which neither injures nor nourishes him, the hidden mineral lying in unseen veins under his feet, are all either unimportant or useless.

The useful is that which makes man's life more easy or more agreeable. But we have agreed, in the hypothesis of the shipwrecked sailor, that Nature by herself supplies us with very few useful things. Excepting the soil which sustains us, the air we breathe, the water we drink, there is nothing which, to my mind, is due to her.

Our first resources, or, more properly speaking, all the gifts of humanity, are the conquests of labour.

Man can neither create nor destroy an atom of matter, yet he can assimilate and identify himself with whatever suits him; he can turn aside whatever menaces him; above all, he can adapt for his use and employ for his profit that which was originally valueless or even dangerous. By means of labour he impresses the stamp of utility upon all he touches, and thus little by little annexes, as it were, the entire earth.

Utility proceeds from and returns to man. If we do not create things themselves, we create their usefulness. But that costs something. Nothing is got for nothing. We are not Nature's spoiled children. After man was created he appears to have been told, "I leave you to yourself. Whatever you produce is your own."

Do you wish to see by some examples how man does his part and becomes the producer of utility?

If, on leaving home an hour hence, you meet a lion at the bottom of the stair, should you hesitate for an instant in regarding it as a noxious animal? Is not this true?

However, thanks to the strenuous exertions of several generations, lions, driven from Europe, have now no abode save Africa. The distance which separates you from them enables you to think of them with indifference.

When an agile, a brave, and skilful man succeeds at the risk of his life in accomplishing the trifling task of lodging a ball between a lion's eyes, the animal is no longer noxious, nor even indifferent and useless. Its skin is worth a hundred francs; it will make a rug.

Suppose that, instead of shooting the brute, a

prudent hunter by means of greater strategy should entrap and imprison it in an iron cage and bring it to Marseilles! The lion disembarked at the dock would fetch many thousand francs.

If, by means of still more skilful and longer-continued labour, a lion-tamer, like Batty, subdues the dread monster, the lion would fetch thirty thousand francs at least. Nature creates a devouring animal: human skill converts it into a bread-winner.

The whole race of domesticated animals in man's service, yielding him eggs, milk, wool, and even flesh, was wild at first, that is to say, was so far separated from, as to be of no use to him. By his skill he not only tamed these animals, but, as it were, he has modified and re-modelled them after a pattern supplied by himself.

Man fashions at will draught horses and racers, oxen for the plough and oxen for the table, sheep which furnish wool and sheep which furnish tallow, fowls which lay eggs and fowls which are fitted for the spit, fat pigs and lean pigs : from one breed of dogs, man has produced the greyhound and the bull-dog, the setter and the harrier, the pointer and the lap-dog. When you go to an exhibition of any sort of live animals, remember that art has as great and Nature as little a share in it as in an exhibition of pictures.

Apply the same method of reasoning to all agricultural, arboricultural, and horticultural exhibitions. Neither our gardens, our fields, nor our woods are masterpieces of Nature, as is ignorantly said; they are masterpieces of human industry.

All double flowers, without exception, are man's work. Pluck a wild rose from a hedgerow, and then go and see a collection of Verdier's roses: you will learn how much Nature has bestowed, and what man has made of it.

All the pulpy and juicy edible fruits are man's work. Man went as far as Asia, and even farther, in quest of the coarse products which resemble our peaches, our cherries, our pears, as much as the wild rose resembles the "Palace of Crystal," or the " Remembrance of Malmaison," rose.

Each of our vegetables represents not only distant voyages, but also centuries of skilled labour and assiduous elaboration.

It was not Nature that gave the potato to the poor of our land. Human industry went in quest of it to America, and has cultivated, modified, ameliorated, varied, and brought it step by step to its present state, accomplishing the result in less than a century. Yet to this century of culture must be added the prior labour bestowed on the plant by the natives of America. When the products of a distant country are brought to us we are prone to believe that Nature alone has done everything. But when the Spaniards discovered America, it had been cultivated from time immemorial. Hence man had turned Nature to his advantage there, as well as in Europe and elsewhere.

Wheat, such as we see it, is not a gift of Nature. It grows spontaneously in Upper Egypt, yet there it yields but a poor and miserable seed, unfitted for making bread. Many ages and a prodigious expenditure of labour were required in order to develop, swell, and perfect the seeds of this useful food for man. Have you ever been told that wheat is distinguished from other cereals by its containing a notable proportion, sometimes a quarter, of nitrogenous substances? This valuable gluten represents the blood and flesh of thousands of generations that perished in the culture of wheat.

While labour supplied the most precious of its useful properties to this grain of which each of us consumes three hectolitres yearly, pharmacy altered the use of fifty vegetable poisons, and converted them to the profit of our species. Not merely does man add a portion of utility to that which possesses none naturally, but he turns bad into good.

During how many ages did the electric fluid hold a place among the number of curses! We knew it only by the dreaded effects of lightning.

Franklin discovered the lightning-conductor, and conferred on everybody the means of neutralizing this great curse. A force, eminently mischievous, becomes indifferent to the man who is prudent and wise. Security during a storm is henceforth the price of easy and inexpensive labour.

But does man halt in so fine a path? No. Hardly has he conquered this hostile power than he undertakes to domesticate it. Lightning, snatched from old Jupiter's hands by Franklin, becomes an instrument of progress. We employ it to transmit our thoughts, to reproduce our works of art, to gild our utensils, and we shall soon make it perform a thousand other services. Before the lapse of half a century we shall see electricity rendered more and more docile, furnishing us with movement, light, and heat, at pleasure.

Will you now study with me how human labour, incessantly multiplied, infinitely increases the usefulness of all our things?

An invisible, disregarded iron mine renders no service to the men who tread upon it.

On the day the geologist, by the travail of his mind, divines this source of useful things beneath our feet, the soil which conceals it gains to some extent an increased value.

When laborious boring has proved the existence

of the mineral, expectation is converted into certainty, and the value of the land is farther increased.

The result of employing labour to work the mine is to bring to the surface some tons of reddish stones containing iron. This matter is not really more useful than the pebbles in the neighbouring stream ; yet it is more valuable, because it is known that things more profitable to man can be extracted from it by labour. The mineral is treated, and the crude metal, which is of greater value, is obtained. The crude metal is refined, and iron is got, which is better. The iron is treated, and, by cementation, it is converted into steel. The steel is wrought, and a thousand things directly useful to man are produced.

The utility of these last products increases in a direct ratio to the amount of labour which men have expended. An anvil weighing a thousand pounds is less useful than a thousand wrought files ; it costs less labour. A thousand pounds' weight of files cost less labour than a thousand pounds' weight of watch-springs ; they contain in themselves a smaller sum of utility. You can easily understand that if the anvil made in a day contained as much utility and was of as great value as a ton of watch-springs, which it took several months to make, everybody would prefer to forge anvils, and no one would weary himself in flattening watch-springs.

Neither a decree, nor a decision, nor a political law has arranged matters in this wise; Nature herself has done it.

It is necessary, indispensable, inevitable, that labour should constantly augment the utility of things, and that men should buy them at the price of greater efforts on learning that they are more useful. Not only is the existence of utility merely relative to man, but it continually varies with our natural or artificial wants.

A stove is useless at Senegal; an ice-making machine is useless at Spitzbergen. In a locksmith's eyes, pincers are objects of first necessity; a duchess has no use for them. On the other hand, a little bonnet, which does not cover her head, is more useful to her than sixty pairs of pincers, for she requires it to drive in her carriage in the Park, and she pays for it accordingly. The agreeable and the useful are perpetually confounded in an advanced state of civilization: I have explained why, in showing that our wants increase with our resources.

Time and distance augment or diminish the utility of our goods. A thing in your hand is of more use to you than if it were ten leagues off. At the distance of ten leagues it is more useful than if it were in America. The greater the distance, the greater is the labour required to enjoy it; you must either pay the cost of carriage or go for it yourself. This fatigue and this outlay are equivalent to the labour that must be expended, for instance, in order to convert iron into steel. A thousand francs in Paris are worth more to a Parisian than a thousand francs in Brussels: a thousand francs in Brussels are worth more than if they were in New York. In like manner a thousand francs which are given you to-day are evidently of greater use than a thousand francs which will be given to you ten years hence. A thousand francs obtainable in ten years are more useful and are worth more than a thousand francs of which the possession is postponed for fifty years. The return may indeed be safe and certainly guaranteed: the question is utility as regards yourself, and you are not sure of living long enough to enjoy a benefit so long deferred.

The utility clearest to all eyes is that residing in material things. Man understands without any effort that a bird in the hand is worth two in the bush, and that it is still more useful when leaving the spit. It is needless to tell you that first the sportsman and then the cook have added a surplus value to the bird. If I put before you a ton of pig-iron, worth fifty francs, and then a ton of fine needles, worth ninety thousand, you will instantly see the enormous supplement of utility which the work of men has added to the metal.

But there are other benefits of which the utility is not as directly visible to our eyes, though it be at least as great. An impalpable, invisible, imponderable idea is often more useful than a mountain of benefits clear to the naked eye. Man is a thinking body; his hands have done much to render the earth habitable, but his brain has done a hundred times more.

Suppose that a great manufacturer had converted a thousand million pounds of iron into steel. Would he have performed as much usefulness in his life as the discoverer of cementation, as he who has put it within the reach of all men to convert iron into steel? He who should transport a mountain ten miles would produce less utility than the discoverer of the lever. For by teaching us a simple law of mechanics we have been put in a position to transport a hundred mountains, if we please, with less outlay and effort. An economy is thus rendered possible which will profit all men who have been and may be born.

If Pascal had said to the men of his day, " I am rich, I possess a hundred miles of pasturage around Montevideo, and a thousand vessels on the Atlantic;

I have caused half-a-million of horses to be transported hither, which I present to you, and which will work for you till their deaths," Pascal would have been less useful to the human race than on the day when, in his study, he invented the wheelbarrow.

Studious men, by a series of discoveries, superinduced the one upon the other, have given to us all the machines which abridge and facilitate labour. England alone possesses a hundred millions of horse-power which work for the profit of thirty millions of men.

The history of civilization may be summarized in nine words.: the more one knows, the more one can perform.

In proportion as science and reasoning simplify production, the quantity of benefits produced tends to increase without augmentation of expense; work done helps the work to be done.

The tools of the human race are nothing else than a collection of ideas. All levers are worn out in the long run, and all wheel-barrows also; steam-engines are not everlasting, but the idea remains, and enables us indefinitely to replace the material which perishes.

It follows from this that the first of useful things for man, is man himself.

3

You are of the greater use to yourself the more you are instructed, rendered better, and, so to speak, more perfect. The development of your personal faculties also enables you to be more useful to others, and to obtain from them greater services through reciprocity.

CHAPTER III.

THE following axiom is one which cannot be repeated to you too often or too loudly: "No man, were he to unite the strength of Hercules to the genius of Newton, can either create or annihilate a grain of matter." I insist on this point because we are all inclined to exaggerate our power and consider ourselves gods. Each time that we happen to invent a roasting-jack or to level a mole-hill, we are puffed up with pride, and we say to ourselves, according to the case, " I have created, or I have annihilated."

Let us be modest and declare in good faith that man's greatest efforts only end in producing an abstraction, utility.

It is not my intention to lead you through the fogs of metaphysics; hence I proceed at once to examples and facts.

The fisherman who dredges a hundred oysters

at the bottom of the sea has not created a single oyster.   However, if he had remained in bed, in place of embarking at daybreak, the hundred oysters would be in relation to us as if they were non-existent.   They would have continued absolutely useless ; it is the fisherman who, by his labour, gives them a new character, appreciable by all men, which is called utility.   He has not then created the oysters, but, in his eyes as in ours, by creating their utility he has done what is equivalent.   In this respect he is a producer.

If all the oysters dredged during the year were consumed on the spot at the seaside, the inhabitant of Paris would concern himself very slightly about their production. ' Oysters, in his eyes, would be use-less things, so long as they were not put within reach for his enjoyment.   Thus the carrier who takes charge of them at Granville in order to bring them to Paris, adds to them a fresh quantity of utility, creates a new utility relatively to the Parisian consumer.   In this sense, he is a producer like the fisherman who has hauled his dredge along the bottom of the sea.   The one has given himself trouble to bring to the surface what was at the bottom, the other has toiled to bring to the south what was at the north.   The oyster woman comes next, and, taking her knife, she adds to the fisherman's and carrier's product a new kind of utility without which you would never have known the taste of oysters. Merely try to open her merchandise yourself, and then dare to say that the honest woman has produced nothing !

All logical labour is productive ; all workers are producers. The fisherman would be a great fool if, as I have often heard it said, he reasoned thus : " The carrier and the oysterwoman are but parasites. They live on my labour ; they work for their benefit a product which I have created." No, my friend, you have created nil ! You have brought near to the consumer a product which was far from him. Another has brought it a little nearer to us ; another has placed it on our table and beneath our fork : all those who have laboured to render your merchandise more useful, are producers by the same title as yourself.

The peasant says, " I have produced an hundred quarters of wheat," and at first sight it appears as if he had gathered this harvest from nothing. He has in reality merely re-united existing elements in the form most useful to man, but which were useless, unfitted for consumption, being dispersed in the air, in the water, in the earth, in the dunghill. He has indeed created the utility contained in the wheat, for this wheat would not have existed as wheat if the good man had not tilled, sown, harrowed, hoed, reaped, and thrashed. But the miller who has produced flour and the baker who produces bread are not parasites of the labourer; they are makers of utility, like himself. The stock-breeder makes oxen in this sense, that he arranges for their birth, watches over their crossing, and supplies them with food. But he has not created an atom of their bodies; he has done no more than superintend the natural phenomenon which transforms five hundred kilogrammes of good green fodder into a kilogramme of meat. He has produced an incontestable sum of utility, that I avow. But the slaughterer who kills the ox and cuts it in quarters; the salesman who retails it in small portions and saves you from buying a whole ox in order to make soup, produce as clear utility as the stock-raiser himself.

To transform a useless thing into a useful one is to produce. To transform a useful thing into a more useful one is to produce. To transport is to produce. To divide is also to produce.

Of these four propositions, the two first do not require to be demonstrated. Every one is of opinion that the hunter, the fisher, the miner, the agriculturist carry on industries which are essentially productive. No one disputes the title of producer to the miller, the baker, the draper, the tailor, the mason, the blacksmith, and those who perform the first, the second, and even the hundredth operation on raw materials.

Half a minute's reflection will enable you to understand that the carrying industry is as productive as any other. Suppose that you are called upon to choose between two loaves of sugar equal in weight, in colour, in savour, but of which the one is ready for you in the grocer's opposite, and the other remains in charge in a Marseilles warehouse. You would not hesitate to choose that which is within reach, and you would think it ridiculous if I asked you why. Why? Because it has a quality the other wants: it is near, the other is distant; it is within reach of your hand, the other is out of sight. This single fact engenders such an increase of utility that you would much prefer giving up a good piece of the one to going in quest of the other. Now, if it is evident that distance makes things lose a notable portion of their utility, you will admit that they are rendered more useful in being brought nearer to you, and that to transport is to produce.

Thus commerce and industry perform a single and similar function despite their different tools and processes. To transport tea from its native China, or to extract lead from its native mineral, is to proceed to the same end by different roads.

Next summer, ice may perhaps be scarce in Paris. Certain persons may manufacture it for you by means of ingenious apparatus; certain merchants may go and procure it for you in Norway. If you had the choice between a kilo of natural ice brought by commerce and a kilo of artificial ice produced by industry, you would take the one or the other indifferently. Industry and commerce would have created for you an identical utility by different means.

The water you use for all the requirements of life cannot be created by any man; yet industry and commerce are equally capable of supplying you with it. Whether a powerful company causes it to ascend to you through pipes prepared for the purpose, whether a humble porter from Auvergne carries it to you for four francs the thousand litres, that have cost him twenty sous, the utility will be the same to you. The wholesale and retail dealer equally bring within your reach a natural thing which abounds in the river, but which, under no pretext, would ascend of itself to your floor.

Must, then, this parasitical water-carrier, who obtains four hundred per cent. from his merchandise, be included among producers? Yes, in truth, and not he only, but all those who retail the goods which we cannot buy wholesale.

It is too evident that, if I possessed a garden near to Monceaux park; if I required fifty thousand hectolitres of water yearly to irrigate a hectare of turf, I should not act so ludicrously as to pay for it two sous the load. In such a case, a stock is procured wholesale.

Wine is bought wholesale, and at the wholesale price, if one has a cellar in which to store it, and if one can pay for a whole barrel. In like manner, the head of an academy who must provide meals for two or three hundred youths, buys a lot of fish at the market and several sheep when sold by auction. But what would become of the artizan, the small tradesman, the unmarried workman, if, at the close of the day's work, he could not make soup without buying an ox, drink a glass of wine without buying a double hectolitre, drink a cup of coffee without paying for a sackful? Retailers, who all carry on the same kind of commerce as the water-carrier, yet without earning four hundred per cent. as he does, render us an immense service. They produce a special form of utility, consisting in putting thirty grammes of coffee within reach of the housewife, who could not pay for fifty kilos, in furnishing him with a chop who could not buy a whole sheep.

So much the better for you if you are rich enough and finely enough housed to be able to dispense with

retailers of all kinds ! But for the large majority of
men, in the existing state of the world, they produce
the most indispensable of all utilities. It is in this
sense that I said above : to divide is to produce.

Yet the list of producers is not exhausted,—it remains for me to establish the following propositions.
To cure is to produce. To teach is to produce. To
please is to produce. To assure is to produce. After
that, I do not despair of proving to you, in opposition to all the declamations of envy, that to lend is
to produce.

Do you grant that among the things useful to
man, the most useful is man himself? Do you accept
the calculations of the economists who say that, commencing at his twenty-seventh year, the individual
reimburses the advances made by society? Do you
think, like J. B. Say and all who reason, that the
problem is not how to beget children, but how to
rear them to man's estate ?

You ought then to acknowledge that the medical
art, by organizing a struggle against the destructive
causes which threaten us from our birth, produces an
incalculable amount of utility on earth. Our life,
according to Bichat's definition, is the aggregate of
the forces contending in us against death. Every
hour, Nature claims the elements of which our body is
composed ; our existence is but a militant loan, in-

cessantly continued and renewed : it would be impossible to rate too highly the fine medical industry
which protects the human being against a universal
conspiring host.

Among the men of your acquaintance, are there
many whom science has not once rescued from
death ? Starting from that point, say whether the
doctor of medicine is a more paltry producer than
the cabinet-maker or the stone-cutter ?

Jean Jacques Rousseau, and all those who have
made mouths water in celebrating the state of Nature, are detestable jesters. For man, the state of
Nature is a state of filth, of privation, of innumerable maladies, and premature death. We still know
a certain number of tribes who live in a state of
Nature. In their case the average duration of life,
in the most genial climates, is from twelve to thirteen years. Among the civilized nations of Europe,
thirty years is the average. Without leaving our
own country, we can recognize a sensible difference
between the life and health of a badly cared for
peasant and of the citizen who dwells close to Dr
Robin and Dr Nelaton.

Having said that, I incline to think you will
not decline to inscribe the Doctor in the first rank
on the list of producers.

If you accord this honour to the men who heal,

you cannot refuse it to the persons who instruct us. I have already said, the more we know the more we can perform. To turn out instructed men is to turn out useful men, and is not he who endows us with the means to be useful, useful. in advance of ourselves?

The following, which I read in a treatise of practical morality, does not fall within my province to judge: " He who plants a tree before he dies has not lived in vain. This is one of the wise sayings of India. The tree will yield fruit, or at the least will afford shade, to those who will be born to-morrow, famished and naked. He who has planted a tree has done well; he who cuts it down and saws it into planks has done well; he who puts the planks together to make a bench has done well; he who, sitting upon the bench, has taken a child on his knee and taught it to read, has done better than all the others. The first three have added something to the common capital of humanity; the last has added something to humanity itself. He has made a man more enlightened, that is to say, better." *

Remember also that the fund of civilization is composed of intangible tools, that is to say, ideas. All the levers existing to-day may be put into the melting-pot; all the drays and wheel-barrows may

* Le Progrès.

be cast into the fire; all the steam-engines may be taken to pieces; all the telegraphs taken down: science, which is the soul of all these useful machines, will survive their destruction, and will replace them in a few days.

Thus head-work, as it is vulgarly called, is at least as productive as the work of the arms. Draw a comparison between a good stout farrier, who shoes twenty-five horses in a day, and a small old shrivelled mathematician who puts figures and formulas on paper, and you will see that the larger producer is not he who hits hard.

That is not all. Sciences and arts produce a moral utility, foreign and superior to their practical applications. Works, of which the effect is to correct our errors, to strengthen our reason, to elevate our spirit, to improve our mind, are as productive in their way as those that tend to lower the price of meat or of bread. The astronomer, the philosopher, the poet, the painter, the musician, the sculptor, do not labour to satisfy the primitive wants of man, yet they satisfy wants as pressing, in the case of the civilized man, as hunger and thirst. In the case of the child of Nature, natural wants are all in all, but we are no longer children of Nature. There is a vast deal of superfluity in our strictest necessaries. We require shoes, shirts, and pocket-handkerchiefs; it is not Nature, but civilization, and a very refined civilization, which forces these necessaries upon us. We stand in need of certitude, of poetry, of music, of painting, of comedy, of a thousand things with which the men who preceded us have dispensed, and with which the great majority of the human species still dispenses in our time. The Parisian who has toiled all day sometimes feels a craving for amusement. In that case, the authors and comedians who amuse him, render him a real service; they quiet his mind, they relax his nerves, they render him more capable of working on the morrow. Pleasure is a useful thing, and he who gives us pleasure is a producer like any other.

When bread costs twenty-five centimes the kilogramme and admission to the Exhibition of the Fine Arts costs a franc, you may see more than a thousand persons give four kilogrammes of bread daily for a promenade of some hours among pictures and statues. On leaving the place, they have consumed with their eyes four kilogrammes of bread. Do they regret this? No; for they breakfasted before coming, they are certain to dine in the evening; the requirement of nourishment is less pressing, at a given moment, than the taste for painting. The visitor who passes through the turn-table of the Exhibition implicitly avows, by giving his twenty sous, that he thinks it more useful to look at the productions of contemporary artists for an hour than to eat four kilogrammes of bread.

When Madame Patti goes and sings in a financier's drawing-room for two thousand francs, she produces, on opening her mouth, a rapid and fleeting utility, but which is none the less valued at two thousand francs by the master of the house, who can reckon. The young and brilliant songstress really produces, in three-quarters of an hour, the equivalent of forty tons of cast metal at fifty francs the thousand kilos. The financier who pays this price for some vibrations of air is not unaware that he could get more work out of forty thousand kilos of cast metal. If he prefer an article which will be consumed as soon as produced, it is because he counts on getting a special form of utility from it ; the pleasure of his guests, a reputation for good taste and splendour, four lines in the newspapers. These advantages, which a gardener of Croissy would not barter for a basket of carrots, are worth two thousand francs in the financier's opinion.

At one time we have seen stalls in the Italian Theatre let for sixteen francs the night, exactly when the hectolitre of wheat fell to sixteen francs. The spectator from the orchestra consumed with his ears the equivalent of a hectolitre of wheat in the course of two or three hours, to wit, the amount of bread an ordinary man consumes in four months. Why does he make such a sacrifice without grudging? Because the special utility produced by the composer, the manager of the theatre, and the performers, satisfies the requirements of his dilettanteism, as a hectolitre of wheat does the hunger of a peasant.

Most economists have a tendency to scorn what is agreeable and deny to it any sort of utility. They forget that utility is always relative to the present wants of man, and not of all men in general, but of a certain man in particular. A roll is more useful than a cigar to the famished unfortunate; a cigar is infinitely more useful than a roll to the stock-broker who rises from the dinner-table.

J. B. Say, who was a most sensible man, but who lived during a rather limited epoch, too readily lessened the utility of pleasant things. He does not admit that the lamps lit in a drawing-room produce the same amount of utility as the lamps lit in a workshop. He insists upon the inutility of lackeys; in general, he is severe upon what he calls the *productions of luxury* and *superfluities;* he believes that nine out of ten fortunes are made by dealing in articles of first necessity.

The truth is, that the lighting of a drawing-room produces a utility of another kind than the lighting of a workshop, but which is absolutely equal in the eyes of the master of the house. If you burn five francs' worth of oil and ten francs' worth of candles on the evening that you entertain your friends, you do not expect that the value of the product consumed will be reproduced under another form in another exchangeable product; yet you pay the same sum, and with as great heartiness, as the manufacturer who furnishes his workmen with light. This is because the pleasure produced by this lighting is equivalent for you, at the time, to any other utility which could be produced by it.

A lackey does less work than a locksmith. To cross one's arms behind a carriage, or to cross one's legs seated in an entrance-hall, that, I admit, is foolish labour whereof the products will never enrich the human race. But does it follow that the lackey is useless to the master who pays him wages? If he did not produce the satisfaction of an artificial and even a ridiculous want, would any one keep lackeys? The master has estimated the product and the cost which a lackey might add to his establishment. The master can reckon; possibly he has worked during forty years of his life, in order to obtain the right of stupidly playing the great man. Nothing prevents my supposing that he has not been a master lock-

smith.   The day he engages a lackey he knows well
that this fellow will not supply the same kind of
service as a journeyman locksmith, but he hopes to
get something else from him.   He says to the lackey,
"My man, I have an income of three hundred
thousand francs, and the custom which governs very
rich Frenchmen condemns me to surround myself
with some well-clad idlers.   This is a want which
has come along with my fortune.   Will you help me
to satisfy it?   Will you undertake not to work in
my service?   You might employ your time in lock-
making; I shall buy it from you, I shall pay you
for all the locks you might have made had you not
been in my service.   Not only will you do no work
yourself, but I shall work for you, or at least I shall
maintain you on the accumulated labour of my life,
so greatly do I rate the service you render in giving
to my entrance-hall a pseudo air of the Faubourg St
Germain!"

In proportion as a people grows civilized and
wealthy, its artificial wants become more numerous
and pressing, superfluity becomes more necessary to
it, and the number of customers for objects of luxury
increases.   And the production of objects of luxury,
from the time of their finding a large enough outlet,
returns enormous profits ; more is to be made out of

the fancies of a single rich man than out of the hunger and thirst of forty poor persons.

It is right to rank with producers all those who, by their industry, avert destruction in assuring the conservation of benefits produced. To assure is to produce.

You know the proverb, One bird in the hand is worth two in the bush. Proverbs are not to be despised ; they nearly always express in the clearest manner a common-sense truth.

A fireproof building is worth more, other things being equal, than a building exposed to all the risks of fire.

Capital shut up in the cellars of the Bank of France is worth more than the same capital exposed without a protector amid the mountains of Calabria.

An undisputed heritage has greater value than if it were in litigation.

Cargo delivered in port represents a larger sum than when upon the deep, exposed to all the chances of the sea.

If you enter a club at two in the morning, with fifty thousand francs in your pocket, your fifty thousand francs are more entirely yours, and consequently are worth more to you, in the streets where the policeman is on duty, than in the plain of Montrouge, where the police are only conspicuous by their absence.

All benefits without exception, human life included, have more value under the reign of law than under the reign of despotism and violence. History makes us acquainted with times and countries where men set but an insignificant store upon their possessions, and poured out their blood like water, so greatly had the despotism of a Tiberius depreciated everything. A hectare of land is worth more in the poorest canton of France than in the most fertile paradise of Abyssinia, because property is as powerfully secured among us as it is feebly secured in that kingdom of Africa.

Among the most civilized nations of Europe, it is easy to prove that a rumour of war, though devoid of foundation, depreciates all the products of labour. Why? Because war, in addition to making ruins everywhere, puts in doubt the things most certainly acquired; there are no abiding properties except in time of peace.

This is why all the men, whose occupation consists in assuring the products of our labour from destruction, are helpers in general production. The advocate who defends your rights, the legislator who defines them, the magistrate who consecrates them, the policeman who avenges them, are producers by the same title as the labourer and city workman. To catch a wolf that devours a sheep nightly is to add thirty sheep monthly to your sheepfold. The soldiers who protect our frontiers against invasion are not parasites, although they live by your labour and mine. The pay we give them is a premium against invasion. We make a bargain with them in which they risk more than we do, for we never sacrifice more than a portion of our incomes, and they frequently offer up their lives.

I do not speak here of *Assurances*, properly so called, because I intend treating them separately. Their object is not to hinder the destruction of products, but to replace them in proportion as they are destroyed.

It remains for me to prove a last proposition, which true economists admit as an incontestable axiom, but which the paradoxical school has denied as well as it could for nearly twenty years. Notwithstanding all that has been said or preached to you on this head, I hope to demonstrate to you with ease that to lend is to produce.

Suppose that a skilled workman or a clever foreman, as may be more or less easily met with in all trades, invents a new process, simpler and more economical than any other. His fortune is made, should he find the means for working his discovery.

Let a hundred thousand francs be given him to establish a factory, and he will be a millionnaire before ten years are over. But meantime he is poor; he has not even the hundred francs required to take out a patent. One of two things must happen; either he will not get credit, and his invention will be lost to others as well as to himself, or a capitalist will advance the hundred francs he needs. In this case, has the lender aided or not to form the fortune that will be made? Yes, for it will be engendered from the marriage of capital to an idea; yes, for the million would have eternally remained in limbo, if no one had made the first advance.

Carry the question into commerce, into agriculture, or wherever you please. A humble clerk in a district feels himself capable of succeeding in a great venture. But to-day he requires money, much money, in order to establish a trustworthy house; the poor fellow has nothing except his salary and his paltry savings. The younger he is, the poorer he is. If no one advances him the necessary capital, he will vegetate in the service of another to the end of his days. The worthy man who intrusts him with a hundred thousand francs, is he or is he not the author of his fortune? Yes, as far as the half is concerned, for if it be correct to say that the hundred thousand francs would not be increased tenfold without the labour of the young merchant, it is equally certain that this well-endowed young man would never have produced a million by his personal efforts without the assistance of the lender.

Observe now one of Grignon's pupils who, from his school days, has exhibited the aptitudes of a distinguished agriculturist. What does he lack in order to employ his talent in a way useful to others and to himself, and to make a small fortune in agriculture? Two indispensable conditions : 1. A lender who will intrust him with a piece of land to cultivate; 2. A second lender who will advance him the capital required to carry on his farm. If no one lends him anything, or if he be lent but one of the two instruments, whether it be the land without the means for tilling it, whether it be the means without the land, all his laudable inclination and his talent will be paralyzed for ever. Is this clear? Would you entirely side with this farmer if, after twenty years of assiduous and successful labour, he said, "I alone have produced the harvests of these twenty years. During twenty years I have sweated from morning till evening on this farm; the landlord has done nothing, he has not even come to encourage us with an inspection. My money-lender has paid as little heed ; the one and the other amuse themselves in the city whilst I work myself to death for them. In virtue of the work which I have done unassisted, whilst the others folded their arms, the returns of this farm ought to belong wholly to me." Being disinterested in this matter, will your good sense allow you to sanction such an argument? Certainly not; you would say to the farmer, "You deceive yourself. Those who have given you the means to produce are producers under another title, but to the same extent as yourself. The first had the power of letting his land lie fallow, since property, in legal phrase, means the right to use or abuse. The second was free to squander foolishly all his capital in eighteen months, as is done by so many fashionable young men; or to leave his money in a chest, and take therefrom the sum needed for his daily requirements. No one would have been able to compel them to act more wisely, for the right of property, as we shall presently explain, is absolute. Thus the capitalist and the landed proprietor have contributed, without leaving their abodes, to the production of your harvests. They have found this answer their purposes, I admit, but you have done so also; and on both sides this was just. They did not lend you their land and their money to serve you, but to serve themselves; and you have not laboured to pay them rent, but to gain as much as possible. All producers produce in virtue of the same principle, that is, personal interest properly understood. The baker does not knead dough in order to feed other men, but to earn his own bread and eat when he is hungry. The mason does not build in order to lodge his neighbour, but to pay his rent."

Yet if to lend is synonymous with to produce, one may thus be at once a producer and idle? Yes. Should you hesitate to take my word for it, here is a personal argument which, I hope, may appear to you unanswerable.

You have produced actively since becoming a man up to your sixtieth year. During these forty years, instead of altogether consuming the fruits of your labour, you have saved a portion, and in this way created a small capital for your old age.

How long will your life last? You do not know, nor do I. When a man has reached sixty, no one can tell where he will stop. Your savings amount to twenty thousand francs, which appears very good indeed, when it is remembered that you accumulated them centime by centime out of very limited salaries or profits. The simple tastes which you have had the sense to preserve will permit you to live on a thousand francs yearly; thus you may, by putting your money into a drawer, provide for your modest existence during twenty years. What if you live to

4

a hundred, as has occurred? Then you must die of hunger, or be shut up in a hospital, there to end your last twenty years, wretchedly.

On the other hand, you have children. They work like you, they earn their living by your example, yet you would not object to transmit to them your small capital. You even think that the money belongs to them in some measure. Why? For two reasons. Firstly, in giving life to them, you have contracted a moral engagement to render their lives as easy as possible, as far as lies in your power. Next, your children have contributed, to a certain extent, in producing your savings. The happiness of being a father, the consciousness of new duties, the desire to see your family prospering, have doubled your energy; you have laboured with greater spirit than if you had been alone in the world. Upwards of a hundred times the thought of your children has shielded you from a piece of useless or harmful expense; you have stopped short on the threshold of the public-house or the café when thinking about your little ones. Hence you would be gratified to find a combination which should assure the repose of your old age for an indefinite period without disinheriting those who are dear to you. Under these circumstances a borrower arrives, and says, "Sir, I can do for you what you require. The small capital you have amassed will, without difficulty, return 10 per cent. in my hands, employed in a sound undertaking. I am not certain about getting my daily bread with the instruments given me by Nature; with twenty thousand francs I should be able to gain two thousand yearly. The half of the return is yours, as is fitting, seeing that you supply me with an indispensable instrument, a tool without which it would be hard or impossible for me to live."

The offer seems a fair one, you close with it. The labour performed comes to the aid of the labour to be accomplished. A man who, without you, would only obtain employment as journeyman or labourer, becomes, by your act, master-workman or merchant. You rejoice to have provided for all your future wants without mulcting of a centime the heirs you love.

Suppose, however, that, twenty years afterwards, your debtor, intoxicated with economical paradoxes, comes to you with all your receipts, and says, "You once lent me twenty thousand francs; I have returned you twenty thousand francs in twenty payments; now we are quits." Your first impulse would be to shout, Stop thief! "No," you would answer, "we are not quits; you have not returned me a centime of what I lent you. I placed at your disposal an instrument of production ; according to our agreement, and in accordance with equity, you have divided the profits with me ; my capital belongs to me. You cannot touch it without being guilty of sacrilege, for these twenty thousand francs are composed of the two most honourable things in the world, labour and the privations of an honest man."

I admit that all kinds of production are not equally laborious. For example, a gentleman's son, who possesses ten houses in a Paris street, works less during the day than his hundred-and-fifty or two hundred tenants. In general, the lender works less than the borrower ; sometimes, he earns as much or even more. To lease land to a labourer is assuredly less hard than to till the land. But we shall explain, when treating of capital, how a man may legitimately inherit the labour of a hundred others, and how the poorest among us are themselves heirs without their knowledge.

For the present, I confine myself to advancing a conclusion which has some importance. This is that a man cannot live on the earth except as a producer.

If you have not found any capital in your cradle, you are condemned to procure the satisfaction of all your wants by personal production. You must make a shelter for yourself, your clothing, your food, and the rest, in one shape or another. A labourer does not fashion his clothes, but he produces grain, all of which he cannot consume himself, and with the surplus he buys clothing; a tailor does not produce grain, but he makes more garments than he uses in his lifetime, and with the surplus he buys bread. Every labourer in the world is in the same case: you may even see jewellers who never in their lives wear a jewel, yet who procure bread, wine, meat, hats, and boots, by means of polishing and cutting precious stones.

The inheritors of work accomplished, or capitalists, cannot secure for themselves a fixed income without placing their capital at the disposal of others, that is to say, by serving without fatigue, but not uselessly, the producers who surround them. Interest compels them to be always lending. The house-proprietor who cannot find tenants is as pinched as a workman out of employment, and for the same reason. He must produce in order to live.

You may tell me that he can sell his property and invest the money produced by it. Yes, but to lend capital or to let houses is always rendering a service, and consequently is to produce. A capitalist who would not oblige any one, and who should elect to spend a portion of his capital daily, would chiefly injure himself. Should I inherit 100,000 francs, an arrangement very moral in itself, and accounted such by the entire human race, enables me to consume every year the twentieth part of my means (that is 5000 francs) without diminishing my small fortune by a sou. To arrive at this result I have but one thing to do, lend my capital to industrious men who have need of it. In this way I have the certitude of enjoying an uninterrupted return to my latest hour, should I live a hundred years and upwards; I am sure of transmitting to my son the patrimony which my father left to me; I have the consciousness of being useful, without moving a hand, and of co-operating towards the production, on a large scale, of good in the earth.

Suppose that, through selfishness carried to the verge of folly, I refuse to place this money at the disposal of other men. I am no longer a producer, and henceforth I shall serve no one but myself. Yet how bad a service! In twenty years I shall be entirely ruined, without having increased my outlay. I shall be wanting in resources at the very moment when I stand most in need of them. My children will accuse me of having annihilated the modest provision for their existence without profiting anybody. Society will blame me for having foolishly destroyed the product of a labour which I did not perform. My conscience will reproach me with having deprived the human race of an instrument of production and wealth. And I shall learn to my cost that the refusal to produce is the suicide of capital.

However, there are men who squander their capital in place of lending it to workers. That is true. There are also madmen, who ascend the Arc de Triomphe and cast themselves down to the ground. Human society cannot always stop these freaks. But when a man is proved to have suicidal mania, he is confined in Charenton. I have seen a good fellow sent there who had no thought of killing himself, but who had lavished a portion of his patrimony along the Champs Elysées. The doctors said that he was smitten with incurable prodigality, and that it was necessary to protect him against his own acts.

The same rigour is not shown to the other mono-maniacs who place their capital in a box or in a hole. These persons, in order to have the pleasure of seeing and handling the precious metals from time to time, retain an instrument of labour in a state of sterility. The passion for heaping up treasure leads to the same result as prodigality. In a country where 100,000 francs, invested at five per cent., double themselves in fourteen years and seventy-five days, the miser who buries that sum in his garden acts with the same folly as the gentleman's sons when they squander 100,000 francs. Only the prodigal consumes in a

year, perhaps in six months, the 100,000 francs
brought forth and acquired, whilst the hoarder takes
fourteen years and seventy-five days to consume with
his eyes the barren money. The result is that the
prodigal has no longer the 100,000 francs he possessed; the miser has but 100,000 when he ought
to have had twice as much; the one has destroyed
100,000 existing francs, the other 100,000 potential
francs: the folly of these two men being finally represented by the same figure.

But the hoarder is less hurtful than the prodigal;
if he hinder his capital from yielding a return, he
at least preserves it in the condition it was received.
And in order to conserve it intact amidst the cease-
less necessities of life, he is obliged to provide for
his wants by personal labour. With ten millions
shut up in your cellar, you will die of hunger amid
this treasure if you do not work in order to live.
The more you determine to hold unproductive capital,
the more are you forced to produce yourself.

Happily, there are very few capitalists who refuse
to lend. Those who prefer to squander, or bury, their
means are the exceptions, and cannot in any case
found a school. The miser's treasure becomes productive upon its master's death. The young madmen who have run through their patrimony are all
engaged in seeking employment, that is to say, use-

ful work. They become producers in spite of themselves, under the penalty of dying of hunger. They then see by painful experience how difficult it is to produce the smallest thing by itself, without the aid of capital, and they bitterly reproach themselves for having destroyed one of these precious instruments.

The entire logic of human existence can be formulated in five words,—"produce in order to consume." Our reason and sense of justice revolt at the notion of a man who should perpetually consume without producing anything. Everybody understands that children should consume on credit : it is right that old persons should end by consuming what they have produced in their prime; it is perfectly proper that the worker should rest when tired, and consume a part of his surplus products. But he among us who should voluntarily live on another's labour, and share useful things without adding to them, would be a true parasite.

CHAPTER IV.

THROUGH an instinct of equity, men do homage to those who have produced more than they have consumed in their lives. Our gratitude to the great producers of all kinds is a very logical sentiment: they have increased the collective heritage of the human race.

We regard with absolute indifference the multitude of those who have consumed the equivalent of their total production: they have lived for themselves, without doing anything for, or against, the interests of the community.

We pity those who, despite their assiduous labour and moderate consumption, never succeed in making both ends meet and who die insolvent. Yet, whether there may have been exaggeration in their outlay or slackening in their labour, blame pursues them in the grave. This is why a good son thinks himself

bound in honour to pay his father's debts. He
desires to purify the name he bears. He says, "My
father has consumed more than he has produced here
below; I must extinguish the deficit he has left,
and restore by my labour the balance he has dis-
turbed."

As for the parasites whose industry consists in
consuming the products of labour, without rendering
anything in return, they are the enemies of the
human race.

There are three classes of parasites—robbers,
beggars, and professional gamesters.

Robbery is an operation consisting in appropri-
ating, by force or cunning, the products of another's
labour. It is the violation of the natural law,
anterior and superior to all positive laws, which confers useful things on their producer. All the things
actually existing on earth belong either to their
authors, or to their authors' assigns. In order to
obtain a portion of them, equity requires that you
should give an equivalent in exchange.

Whoever appropriates a roll costing a sou, without giving a sou for it, does injury not to the baker
alone, but to the whole human race; he consumes
another's labour without furnishing an equal amount
himself. The loss is insignificant in itself amidst a
society so rich as ours; but it is precisely in rich

societies that robbery is least excusable, on account
of the facilities for earning a livelihood being most
numerous. Where the slightest service performed
to the rich by the poor, the opening of a door, the
offer of a light, is recompensed by a sou and upwards, the robbery of a sou is equivalent to an in-
solent refusal to serve other people.

To rob a poor man is more odious than to rob a
rich man, but it is neither more nor less criminal.
A prejudice, not yet uprooted from among us, considers him half innocent who steals five francs from
a millionnaire, and three-fourths innocent should he
filch a louis to the detriment of the State. The
truth is, that all violations of the right of property
are equally culpable. Whether rich or poor, all
the men who work on the surface of the globe are
wronged by any robbery whatsoever. The workers of Austria, and of the United States, are as much
interested as ourselves in repressing robbery in
France : hence extradition treaties between civilized
nations. Two States might go to war without these
treaties being suspended, so much superior in interest
is the repression of robbery to the causes which set
nations at variance. The main point is to maintain
and confirm this principle of universal justice : the
product belongs to the producer.

Astonishment is sometimes shown at the courts

inflicting the same punishments in cases where the robberies amount to a million and to one hundred francs. Why is it that a magistrate whose conscience is so scrupulous in establishing the quality of a robbery, appears indifferent as to the quantity? Because the quantity stolen, were it a million, is but a trifle compared with the moral injury which affects humanity as a whole. The robbery of a million francs, or the robbery of a sou, if unpunished by law, would depreciate all the products of labour to an equal extent. We value our goods in proportion to the security which surrounds them. If you were only half certain to possess your watch undisturbed, of which the value is one hundred francs, it would not be worth more than fifty. Laws are framed in consideration of public security. They punish domestic robbery with severity, in order that the man of means may know himself to be protected against the easiest of all crimes; they make a distinction between the robber by day and the robber by night, the robber unarmed and the armed robber, the robber within doors and the robber who enters through the window, the robber who finds a key in the lock and the robber who picks the lock or breaks it open, because general security is endangered to a greater extent by the existence of evil-doers more daring, more violent, and more experienced.

The exact amount of the goods which have passed from one hand to another is but a secondary question, if the smallest ascertained robbery diminishes the value of all existing riches till the capture of the culprit.   Among the consequences following a · robbery, there are two which it would not be right to omit, because they directly affect social economy :

Stolen goods are goods lost.

Stolen goods are corrupting.

Nothing is truer and more philosophical than the old common saying, "Property wrongly acquired never profits." An honest workman cleaves to his earnings as to his eyes. They are the prize of his toil. He has risen early six days running ; he has assiduously laboured ten hours daily, sometimes longer. He has spent his breath and the sweat of his brow; on receiving his wages he can say without exaggeration, I have taken it from my own body ; it is my flesh and blood ; I have been coining money all the week and this is what I have produced. He delays returning home to display his small gain before his wife's eyes. While walking along, the silver coins jingle from time to time, and it gives him pleasure to hear the sound. Perhaps he may even once or twice slap his pocket to arouse the dormant money. If an evil-doer watches his path in order to dispossess him of his money, he will meet with his match. The honest man becomes a lion in defence of his modest earnings.

Do not fear about the money being well employed. It will pay for the bread, meat, and soap of the household, and the school fees of the children. Something will be put aside as a provision for the rent. The surplus, if any, will go to pay for clothing; if nothing be required at the moment, the Savings' Bank is but two steps off. Excellent money! honest money! you render moral whoever fingers you. This man will carefully refrain from squandering you in debauchery; he knows too well, by experience, how much it costs to obtain you.

In course of time a portion of the wages is converted into good linen, into wearing apparel, into plain but serviceable furniture. Another portion has transformed the children into small men, who know more than their father, and who, in consequence, will be able to select a less severe form of labour. The rest is invested in the funds or in shares. That may not amount to a large figure, but it is the beginning of capital, the germ of a humble fortune. If the father, or one of his sons, wishes to set up on his own account, this money will permit him to make the venture.

The author of all these things regards that which

surrounds him with legitimate pride. "All that," he thinks, "is my handiwork. From my Sunday coat up to my children's education, I have paid for everything by my toil." Not an article of furniture in his narrow lodging fails to recall to him a piece of drudgery, some months of privation, long and patient saving. The wife, who has worked in concert for twenty years with this man, is still prouder than he. The children are respectful and grateful. Trained in so good a school, they work, they economize, they begin to repay the debt of their education. If a misfortune, which must be foreseen, should condemn them to inherit all this to-morrow, I pledge myself they will accept their parents' savings as a relic. I do not know whether they succeed in doubling the sum, but, assuredly, they will not go and drink it at the public-house.

The successful and daring robber, who has made one hundred thousand francs at a stroke, appears to you rich at first sight. It seems that in passing from one chest to another this capital has been in no wise lessened. In fact, if the evil-doer could go to a stock-broker and take one hundred thousand francs' worth of shares or debentures, the capital would have changed hands without being diminished by a fraction.

But the robber's first care is to hide a portion of

his money; the second, to squander the remainder. Why should he hide it? For a hundred reasons. In the first place, because he dreads justice, lest the money found upon him should be an element in convicting him. Next, he probably has accomplices; if he must share it with them, he will no longer have one hundred thousand francs, but fifty or twenty-five, according to their number. The small portion he retains hangs heavily on his hands; he hastens to expend it as soon as possible, firstly, to ease his mind, secondly, to get rid of it.

Money has less value in his eyes than in those of an honest man, because he is not certain of retaining it, because he has not laboured to acquire it, because he thinks that he can steal more when he has expended what he has.

The necessity of concealment excludes him from secure, regular, and useful investments. He would not appear before a banker for anything in the world, with this sum in his hands. Fear drives him to low haunts where an entire population of inferior parasites lies in wait to pluck him. An asylum is sold to him, secrecy is sold to him, forgetfulness in an orgie is sold to him, and this capital, which in honest hands might become a very fine instrument of labour, soon melts away and runs off in filth among the thousand slums of Paris.

I have spoken of an exceptional, improbable robber, who obtains at a stroke one hundred thousand
francs of coined gold.   But, ninety-nine times out of
a hundred, the wrong-doer's profit is less clear, less
available, and less easy to realize.   Since the march of
enlightenment has extended the practice of economical payments, hardly any one keeps sums of money in
his house.   If the celebrated Cartouche ventured to
rise from the dead in Paris, he would scarcely find
anything else to take than shares and personal
articles.

Registered shares are surrounded with such pre-
cautions that they can never benefit an illegitimate
possessor.   Thus a clever rascal prefers to burn them
on the spot rather than to try and sell them.   The
capital represented by the papers he has destroyed
remains intact and does not change hands.   But the
security of the rightful proprietor is destroyed, and
his enjoyment interrupted for a longer or shorter
time.   He always has his capital, but he does not
possess it; he has the right to certain returns, but he
cannot deal with it till an arrangement be made; a
part of his means is, so to speak, realized by the robbery.

Shares to bearer are more easily negotiated; but
as the loser, if he be clever, can stop them by giving
notice, a robber who knows his business fights shy

of such compromising goods and destroys them pro-
miscuously with the registered certificates. There
again a little paper only is really lost; the capital
subsists and does not change hands, but the legitimate proprietor is condemned to troublesome and
laborious courses which embitter his possession without profit to any one. Among documents payable to
bearer, bank notes are assuredly the most conveni-
ently negotiated : inexperienced scoundrels imagine
that they can dispose of them with impunity, like
gold and silver, but they deceive themselves. Each
note has a letter and number which give to it a kind
of individuality and enable it to be recognized among
a thousand. By means of a very simple precaution
which is within the reach of all holders, a note may
become a means of detection and lead the robber before the assize court. Therefore, nothing is more
sensible than the distrust which depreciates all these
papers in skilful evil-doers' eyes and makes them
prefer money, furniture, merchandise.

But furniture and merchandise lose the greatest part
of their price by falling into the hands of a wrongful
possessor. If the robber alters them, if he transforms
a collection of medals, a piece of jewelry, into ingots,
he literally annihilates all the surplus value which
man's labour had added to the precious metals. A
considerable amount of capital perishes yearly in this

way and is lost to the world. ∴ The articles resold in
the state they were when stolen, are depreciated by
this alone, that they become second-hand goods: the
same piece of cloth which was worth one hundred
francs in the manufactory, is not worth more than
fifty in a shop in the Temple or at a pawnbroker's
auction. Add to this waste the depreciation due to
the receipt of stolen goods. The receiver being the
robber's accomplice and running the same risks,
logically demands to share the profits of the crime;
he does not hesitate to offer for a perfectly new piece
of merchandise the quarter or the tenth of its value
in the warehouse. When he has robbed the robber,
he becomes his substitute, so to speak; he feels the
same dread of justice, the same scorn for an article
obtained at a low price, the same eagerness to get rid
of it. He seeks and finds purchasers among a
public on the verge of honesty, which is demoralized
by the touch of goods wrongfully acquired.

The proceeds of robbery corrupt all who handle
them. You may meet persons who think themselves
irreproachable when paying a louis for that which is
worth double or treble. If they reason a little they
will understand that great bargains, carried to a certain limit, render the buyer the receiver's accomplice; but they will not argue. They proudly display their purchases and boast of having paid less

than their value for them. They consider that this perturbation of commercial and industrial laws is due to their lucky star, or is a triumph of their sagacity. Opportunity makes more thieves than is supposed. It is in this sense that I can say, "Stolen goods are corrupting."

Beggars are not robbers, excepting when they combine the two trades, which sometimes happens. But nearly all professional beggars use fraudulent tricks in order to obtain a part of another's fortune. In appearance, the part is infinitesimal, but it is considerable if all the sums uselessly absorbed by mendicity were added together.

The sham wounded, the sham sick, the sham mothers who bemoan a buried child, or press a newborn cardboard babe to their breasts ; the sham workmen out of employment who have never employed their ten fingers ; the sham poor who have share certificates in their desks, are so many parasites who trade on the simplicity of worthy souls.

Our laws punish the man who causes a thousand persons to hand over to him a hundred thousand francs on one pretext or other. ' He is liable to imprisonment of from one to five years and a fine amounting from fifty to three thousand francs. The persons injured may institute actions at law and call upon the courts to make good the sums taken out of their pockets.   It would appear monstrous to us that this wrongfully gotten fortune should be transmitted to the heirs of the swindler.   But, when we read in the newspapers that a beggar on a particular bridge or at a certain church has left one hundred thousand francs in a mattress, the fact appears to us as simply curious; we think it just and natural that the children or next of kin of this ingenious old man should divide the spoils of his dupes.

Society has never thought fit to put an embargo on a particular estate and say, "This money, the product of labour, has been fraudulently diverted by a man who does not work; we will take possession of it and divert it to help those who labour."   Is mendicity therefore a recognized industry among civilized nations?

The enriched mendicant may reply to that, "I have taken nothing; everything has been given me. Does money belong to those who acquire it?   Have they the right to use and abuse it?   May they apply it indifferently to useful works and in honourable and agreeable liberality?   The hundred thousand francs I possess have been given to me copper by copper gratuitously.   I have not had recourse to fraudulent tricks, I have not promised my benefactors to render their alms a hundredfold: I have been clothed with rags, I have sat on a stool; the charity

of worthy souls has done the rest." " Yes, but the
charity of worthy souls would not have given you so
many small coppers had it not been supposed that
real destitution was being alleviated. If you had
only admitted you had a fortune of one thousand francs
the other ninety thousand would not have been given
to you. Among those who have enriched you, how
many were, and are, still poorer than yourself? The
rags, the stool, the outstretched hand, all the repre-
sentation of poverty, constitute a fraudulent trick.
You have made use of a false quality in passing
yourself off as poor when you were not so."

I admit, however, that mendicity would become
excusable in the eyes of economists if the sham poor
often left at their death a capital of one hundred
thousand francs. Their falsehood, condemned by
morality, would finally terminate in a useful result.
What is a copper to him who throws it into the
beggar's bowl? Next to nothing; whether he gives
or keeps it, he will be none the richer or poorer.
Two millions of sou pieces spread over two millions of pockets represent but a sterile, inert good ;
money, thus subdivided, returns nothing for lack of
cohesion. Gather together these particles and you
will have a sum, a capital, an instrument of labour.
He who, by an honest process, should extract two
millions of sous from two millions of pockets in

order to create a capital of one hundred thousand francs, would render society a service, like the skilful metallurgist who should gather together the 100 kilos of iron dust scattered in the streets, therewith to make a powerful lever.

But pauperism ends precisely in an opposite result. Saving some exceptions, beggars squander daily the product of their dismal harvest. Money cast to them by charity does not remain in their hands; it goes straightway to the public-house and to the most disgusting debauchery. Beggars are nearly all spendthrifts, and how could they be otherwise? Man lays store on his goods in proportion to the labour they have cost him. Those who have got money without doing anything, those who count upon always getting it in the same way, are not prone to save, either from inclination or reason. Wherefore should they deprive themselves of anything, seeing they have an inexhaustible mine to work? For what purpose should they form an instrument of labour, when they have resolved never to produce anything, when they know that society is always ready to toil for them?

These parasites marry, multiply, and found a stock of parasites. Their children are naturally disposed to imitate their father and mother; they are not taught the nobility of labour; from birth they arc habituated to shame. They are a sad and baneful brood, absorbing in certain countries more than a tenth of what is produced without making any return.

Does begging create almsgiving, or does almsgiving give rise to begging? Each does its part. We are in a vicious circle. I have dwelt in succession in the part of France where the most is given to the poor, and the part of Italy where charity lavishes its larger alms. At Quimper, as at Rome, my first care was to search by what miracle so much money spread abroad had increased distress instead of curing it. At Rome, as at Quimper, the wisest and best people replied to me, " It is quite simple ; the more you water weeds the more abundant their growth."

If no one had the lamentable courage to hold out a hand in the streets, no one would dream of giving a penny to the idler who had not earned it. But, if all the producers agreed to refuse the toll to those who refused to produce, all able-bodied persons would consider it a duty to earn their own livelihood and there would be no more begging.

Do you wish to manufacture beggars by the hundred? Open your window and throw a franc to all those who come and sing, or grind organs before you, in the street or the court. On the morrow you will be visited by all the professional beggars ;

5

before a week is over fifty persons in your district, who have not yet begged, will desire to profit by the alms, and the evil of mendicity will spread from neighbour to neighbour like an epidemic, Heaven only knowing where it will end.

There are villages in Italy, and even in France, where children run after strangers, asking for coppers. The stranger gives a copper and thinks he acts the great man : he never fancies he is the corrupter of these childen. Among us the modern spirit is strong enough to combat and cure this vice of education; yet I shall never forget that in 1858, in the province of Loretto, peasants left their harvest, which was splendid, to come and beg from us. I turned to one of them and asked him how he had the face to beg on the border of his own field ? He replied, " Sir, I have never missed doing so from my earliest child-hood; and as I have always got something, I continue doing so." " But, if you are not ashamed to beg, why do you work ? " " Because the other trade does not yield enough. You may be sure that if travellers would give me sufficient to live upon, I would never use my ten fingers."

I remember in the avenue of Neuilly, one evening, between five and six o'clock, being hampered with a newspaper I had just read, so I offered it to two masons leaving their yards. My argument, very

logical in its way, was this: "I have got all I want
from the newspaper; it may still instruct or inform
several people; if I throw it away, it will be dirtied
and lost." But one of the two passers-by gave me a
salutary lesson by saying, "If I desire to read a
newspaper, I shall pay for it out of my wages; you
owe me nothing." Assuredly, that honest man had
never in childhood begged upon the high road running through his village.

In pointing out the defects of badly organized
charity, our aim is not to preach an opposition go-
spel, and to forbid the rich to do good. The simple
point is to show that almsgiving exercised without
the greatest circumspection runs exactly counter to
its object.

It is praiseworthy and necessary that all workers
should join together to succour children, the aged,
the sick, all those who cannot earn their bread by
working for themselves. Doubtless the day will come
when individual foresight and thrift will render hos-
pitals and almshouses useless, but, till then, public
benevolence and private charity have a noble task to
perform.

What social economy combats like a pest is the
pauperism of the able-bodied men who are maintained
by blind charity. The commonness of gratuitous gifts
has elevated destitution into a profession; it has cre-

ated hereditary pauperism. Not only are there beggars at fixed places, installed at a particular part of
the public highway, and who transmit their establishment like a stockbroker's or notary's office, but among
those who are rather improperly styled shamefaced
poor, there are dynasties of idlers who have gone
through the occurrences of 1789 and 1793 without diminution of income; their fixed, invariable
revenue is inscribed in the great book of public
sensibility.

I notify the abuse and yet I dare not say, end it.
The question is very complex, for, indeed, to all good
rich people, giving is a pleasure, almost a necessity.
Each time we put our hands in our pockets to succour a true or feigned, a merited or an unmerited unfortunate, we become elevated in our own eyes. Social
economy exclaims, " It is right to receive the equivalent of what we give." The heart replies, " It is
sweet to give without receiving."

Reasoners and calculators are in the right when
they tell us: " A million divided among 400,000 persons gives 2 francs 50 centimes to each. This is nearly
what each one of those who are assisted would earn in
a day, if he worked. To give a piece of bread to an
able-bodied man, capable of earning it, is to weaken
the great and holy law, " In the sweat of thy
face shalt thou eat bread." ' This is to deprive

society of the services which this man might render
it by labouring. To give to those who toil, whether
by buying their work above its value, whether by
letting them have commodities below the price they
should fetch, is to disturb the equilibrium of industry
and wrong the majority of workers, by creating unequal competition to the profit of particular persons.
Those whom you oblige will be able, by this alone,
to vend their products at a reduced price and thereby
to kill the labour of others.

In short, charitable operations crumble away,
without profit to society, the instrument which might
have become useful. A million daily, a milliard every
three years, is given away in France, and of this
amount of capital, which might be multiplied in industry to the profit of all workers, not a centime remains. The lever falls into dust, and that is the
end of it.

Nothing is more exactly true than this sombre
picture. Does it follow that the men who are really
charitable should stand with folded arms in presence
of the spectacle of distress? No. The best among us
will continue to give alms, so long as this palliative
shall not be replaced by the right substitute for the
evil.

But, unless I deceive myself, the remedy has
been discovered. In our day, in our midst, the

ingenious charity of a woman has solved the most frightful of social problems. In order to extinguish the parasitical mendicity which trades upon the rich without profit to the poor, it is sufficient to modify, in conformity with the modern spirit, the touching axiom, " He that hath pity upon the poor lendeth to the Lord." How has it been altered ? By teaching little children another formula quite as fine and far more practical, as follows : " Who lendeth to the poor giveth to God." It does not enter into my plan to examine in detail the rules of a particular charitable institution, but I can vouch that the Society of the Prince Imperial is founded on a principle which is a complete revolution, and one of the happiest.

Around you there are millions of worthy fellows who are very industrious, very intelligent, and very estimable, who have never begged, but who have more than once been reduced to great straits, because their only instruments of labour are their arms, and because manual labour of that kind yields a return which is insufficient, unequal, and precarious. Lend them with discernment that which you throw at hazard among the begging and moaning tribe of parasites. Do not lend except for a fixed period: the most meritorious will refuse this disguised form of alms.

Ought the loans to be made without interest, or

on favourable rates ? For my own part I do not
think so, and for the following reasons. In a
country where the regular rate of interest is five per
cent., 100 francs, payable on the 1st of December,
1872, will exactly represent 105 francs payable on
the 1st of December, 1873. The two figures, unequal in appearance, are equal in reality, if the time
be taken into account, and there is not a mathematician who would challenge this proposition : 100
francs to-day are equal to 105 francs in a year.
Thence it follows, that to lend 100 francs without
interest for a year is equivalent to giving five francs
to the borrower. To lend 100 francs at three per
cent. is to give two francs to the borrower, if the
average rate of interest be maintained at five per cent.,
during the whole year. Between friends, considerable
sums are lent without taking account of interest ;
but it is perfectly understood that the borrower
receives a present, that he is under an obligation to
the lender, and that, after having repaid the exact
amount of the loan, he owes him a surplus payable
in good offices. This obligation has the defect of
being badly defined. Of two friends, one of whom
has gratuitously obliged the other, the first is inclined to exaggerate the importance of the service
rendered ; the second very soon revolts against this
kind of servitude, and a quarrel often ensues on

account of a gratuitous loan having been offered and accepted.

Between men of business, the creditor who has lent 100 francs on good security and the debtor who has returned 105 francs at the end of a year, are quits. They have reciprocally rendered services of equal value. The first has obliged the second by making over to him the use of 100 francs for a year ; the second has obliged the first by giving him five francs in excess of the 100 francs received. The gratitude due on both sides is paid off and extinguished. There is neither benefactor nor debtor, neither patron nor client.

With what object has modern benevolence substituted loans to labour for gifts to idleness? It is not in order to change the form of alms, but to abolish them. The thought which inspired this generous revolution never intended retaining the poor under a skilfully disguised form of patronage. The design is to emancipate the very persons who are helped, and to render them at once happier and more independent. In a social state, having equality as its basis, the noblest benevolence is that which permits those in want to ameliorate their own condition themselves without being indebted to anybody.

This interesting work is but in its infancy ; the

period of discussion is not ended, and as the best spirits of our time unite together in the quest of improvement, I have thought it right to indicate what, according to my personal opinion, seems most advantageous and most just.

It is right that the indigent, when they borrow in order to work, should pay the same rates as everybody else. They may be freed from paying interest, which may be added to the capital, but it is not fitting that a present should be made of it. Competition being the law of commerce and industry, those who are assisted ought not to have as a privilege the gratuitous use of capital; they would thereby contend too advantageously with those who borrow an instrument of labour at five or six per cent.

To society, it is important that the capital subscribed for the work of regeneration should gradually increase and extend its benefits year after year until pauperism shall be totally extinguished.

It is advantageous to the borrower to pay interest on the capital lent to him. By returning his instalments he proves to others and to himself that he is not a parasite, one of those who receive without making return. This sentiment makes him grow in power and dignity, the moral spring of his mind is strengthened, and the amelioration of his whole being compensates for the economy of five per cent. he might make in accepting the interest as alms. He holds his head higher, he thinks with more independence, he is more of a man. Can it be said that he is absolved from all gratitude towards the generous creditors who have put a tool into his hands? No, for a loan has been made to him, under entirely moral guarantees, at the same rate as if he had been able to offer the best security. The poor person who has only two arms is subject to the alternative of being refused all credit, or of borrowing on frightful terms, for the disposal of capital is the more onerous the less the chances are of repayment.

The benevolent loan is in other respects more laborious and difficult than the free gift; it requires a hundred times more reasoning and consideration. To find money is nothing in such a country as ours; but to distribute it well necessitates an appeal to the highest sagacity and the greatest devotedness. Before lending a poor person one thousand francs it is requisite to weigh his morality, his intelligence, his aptitude for business. The slightest error in this diagnosis leads to the loss of the sum, and compromises the noblest experiment ever made by the genius of charity. Oh, how much simpler and easier would it be to give a sou to the first beggar you meet without caring about what he does with it!

But if this new charity requires more labour, it will bear other fruits. The gift to idleness has been in operation for centuries; it has only produced poverty; the loan to labour, began yesterday, has already made some men happy and independent.

It remains for us to speak of the last class of parasites—professional gamesters. But, as it is impossible for a gamester to be always successful, as money got by gaming, having cost no labour, melts away quicker than any other, as it is almost unheard-of that a fortune acquired by gaming is preserved, as all professional gamesters, with the exception of some phenomenal persons who can be cited, have ended badly, this category of unproductive men may be transferred to that of robbers or mendicants.

As a pastime, play is a minor contract which is perfectly honest. Two labourers, in the evening, after a well-filled day, take away a portion of their wages and reciprocally part with it under a condition. For example, the five francs I have put on the table are yours. I give them beforehand. I put you in possession of all my rights to this piece of money if you score five points at ecarté before me. You, on your part, dispossess yourself beforehand, in my favour, of a like sum, if I score the first five points.

In this there is neither production, nor consumption of wealth, but the displacement of some five-franc pieces which leave one pocket to enter another.

However, I request amateur players to note two things :—

First. Admitting the absolute equality of the chances, the player always runs the risk of losing more than he can win. If you have ten louis in your pocket, and if you think fit to stake one of them ; in case of loss, you diminish your means by a tenth ; in case of winning, you but increase them by an eleventh.   Second. Twenty francs won at play have less value than twenty francs lost, and one is deceived in saying that Peter puts into his pocket all that comes out of the pocket of Paul.   Paul has lost the precious money of labour ; Peter has only won the money of chance, which makes a notable difference in practice.

CHAPTER V.

EXCHANGE.

If the first economic law be the obligation to produce, the second is the necessity of exchanging.

The workman might well manufacture products in unlimited quantity; if he had not the means of exchanging them for others, he would be terribly destitute. A hundred thousand hectolitres of grain are a property not to be despised, but they would not hinder you from dying of cold in winter if you did not exchange a portion for clothing, for combustibles, and a dwelling. A hundred thousand stères of wood would not hinder you from dying of hunger; one hundred thousand barrels of claret would not help the wine grower to traverse the distance which separates Bordeaux from Paris; but a few litres of good wine given in exchange for a railway ticket would transport him in a day without fatigue.

A mason can build a house for himself, a tiller of

the soil can procure for himself grain, wine, tobacco, hops, meat, according to the land he culti- vates and the climate he dwells in ; a waggoner can transport himself quickly from one point to another ; a tailor can make clothes for himself. But in order that the same man should have at once lodging, liv- ing, clothing, means of transport, and all the neces- saries of life, he must incessantly exchange his products for those of other mén.

The workman who says with legitimate pride, " I am self-sufficing," what does he mean by these words ? Does he profess to have himself created all the pro- ducts he uses ? No ; but he boasts, and rightly too, of producing a sufficient quantity of exchangeable goods to satisfy all his wants.

Strictly speaking, it is possible that an isolated indi- vidual might imperfectly provide for his most press- ing needs, during a certain time, without exchanging anything with another. Certain savages live in this way, under a benignant sky which reduces man's wants almost to nothing. They act as hunters, fishermen, builders, cooks, tailors, and shoemakers, for their personal purposes. But their aptitude in doing everything hinders them from excelling in any. They know too many trades to be able to do one well. When they have turned their hands to everything in one day, the product of their labour does not represent the sum of useful things which an English or French working man would produce in an hour. Thus they rush to avail themselves of exchange, from the moment civilization comes within their reach: they hasten to offer their products in order to obtain ours, and we gain by the bargain, in selling to them our labour of one hour for their labour of a day or more.

Simple good sense explains to you the superiority of civilized labour over savage labour. The first condition for producing much, speedily, and well, is to specially stick to the business one can perform the best. The best endowed apprentice commences as a pure blunderer; in time, by application and practice, he attains to getting as much as is possible out of his arms and tools. But, if we succumbed to the foolish ambition of doing everything ourselves, life would be only a long and deplorable apprenticeship.

The performance of a single thing develops surprising aptitudes in an individual. The carpenter, the joiner, the farrier, acquire in a few years the sureness of hand which you have doubtless admired, if you have watched them rather closely. A skilful coachman driving through the crowded streets of London or Paris, shows you what being accustomed to a particular work can add in precision to the sight, and decision to the mind. A professional accountant plays with figures; an old sergeant, acting as instructor, juggles with his rifle; a good schoolmaster moulds and shapes like wax the rebellious brain of forty youths; a sailor runs along the yards amidst a gale; a slater, a fireman, run over roofs; a professional improvisor will dictate a hundred verses on the spur of the moment, or speak for four hours in succession.

From the top to the bottom of society you see a multitude of men and even women who excel in an art or a trade, from having been specially engaged in it from infancy. Have you never admired the memory, the nimbleness, and the dexterity of restaurant waiters? And these valuable domestics (some still exist) who wait without embarrassment or noise at a dinner of twelve people? All useful or agreeable talents are the fruit of special training.

It is admitted that a good amount of general instruction is the counterpoise of special training, otherwise the worker would be nothing but a machine. It is still to be desired that, in view of dull times and other accidents, every producer should add a second string to his bow: this is a precaution which cannot be recommended too strongly to the workmen who live by ministering to luxury. But the beginning of wisdom is to choose a means of earning a livelihood, to have a speciality, to concentrate all one's talents and powers upon a principal end. For the individual who considers himself a jack of all trades is a savage astray amid civilization ; he lives and dies worthless.

The earliest exchange was doubtless contemporaneous with the first work, that is to say, this mechanism is as old as man himself. No progress in any department could be achieved here below, if each individual had been compelled to learn all the arts essential to existence. The mere fact of exchange has created an organization of labour far superior to all those which reformers (or those who are so called) have sketched in recent days. It may be here summarized in a few lines.

The individual can count upon wanting nothing should he produce a certain amount of useful things, it matters not what. Even when he creates nothing for his personal use, he is certain of procuring whatever is necessary and something more, provided he supplies a quantity of labour useful or agreeable to other men. He may then, in choosing an industry, deduct from the variety of his wants and reduce the whole problem of his existence to this question : Of what am I capable ? Among all useful products, what one am I best fitted for furnishing ?

Children are disposed to believe that it is necessary to be a confectioner in order to have plenty of sweetmeats to eat, and that the shoemaker must be better shod than other men. Experience does not take long to teach them that, thanks to exchange, the largest quantity of any article may be obtained by producing the largest quantity of another article, whatever it be.

Producers who live and die without having consumed one of their products are numbered by millions. The vintagers of Clos Vougeot drink common claret, the workmen of Alfred and Humann get their clothes at the Bell-Jardinière or even at the Temple; the Lyons' weavers do dress their wives in silk. On the other hand, a large manufacturer of chintz has his drawing-room hung with brocatelle; a manufacturer of hardware for exportation scorns the products of his factory; a dealer in common china eats off Sèvres porcelain. The most precious products abound around the man who produces most utility; the humblest fall to the lot of the man who produces the least, whatever be his department of industry. A stonecutter does not dwell in a stone house: he is too well pleased if plaster and brick give him a tolerable shelter. As to a diamond-cutter, he might live a hundred years without the notion occurring to him of wearing his products as waistcoat buttons.

In all these facts there is an apparent contradiction, of which ill-intentioned rhetoricians have often made use. When workmen were less enlightened and less sensible than at present they were told: It is unjust that fine clothes should be worn by men who cannot sew; it is monstrous that the workwoman dressed in cotton should cut out, and stitch, silk gowns for a banker's wife. Tirades have been published about the poor diamond-cutter who has not even a diamond ring to put on his finger on Sunday.

These old pieces of declamation will appear to you in their full absurdity if you recall, firstly, that all useful things properly belong to him who has produced them, or his assigns; secondly, that to get a portion of them, large or small, equal value must be given in exchange; thirdly, that the value of labour is proportioned to the quantity of utility produced, whatever be the materials employed. Gold is fifteen and a half times more precious than silver, but the skilful chaser, who adds by his labour the value of twenty-five louis to the kilogramme of silver, will receive for it twenty-five golden louis; whilst a turner of common articles will receive four francs ten sous in silver for having chased gold watch cases. Truffles are worth three hundred times more than potatoes, but the agriculturist who should produce ten thousand sacks of potatoes in a season would have the right to eat truffles, while the truffle-hunter who should find but three or four kilos a month would eat nothing but potatoes.

The workman is entitled to the whole surplus value which *he himself* has added to things. Manufactured products, like a black coat, a silk gown, a diamond ornament, do not reach the consumer till after having passed through a multitude of hands all of which, in turn, add an additional value. It is just and natural that each of the workmen should exchange the utility he has produced, for an equivalent. The agriculturist, who furnishes the first element in a black coat, is entitled to the price of the wool; the merchant, who traverses the country to collect the wool from several farmers, is entitled to the price of his exertions; the carman, who conveys the bales to the manufactory, is entitled to the price of his journey; each of the workmen who remove the grease, card, dye, spin, weave, press, comb the cloth, becomes, so to speak, the creditor of the merchandise, and acquires a right proportionate to the value added to it.   -

Six hundred grammes of fine wool, worth three francs at the outset, furnish at last a black coat which, if well made, is worth as much as 125 francs. The day the consumer gives 125 francs in exchange for this coat, he pays in a lump the initial value of the raw material and all the increased values which have been successively added by a hundred workmen. The coat, when paid for, owes nothing to any one.

But, if one of the hundred producers who have had a hand in the work should appropriate the whole, he would wrong ninety-nine others. If the farmer were to take it and say, "This is my wool!" or if the journeyman tailor were to pull it away, saying, "This is my stitching!" all the others would exclaim, "Stop thief!" In order that each of those who had helped to make the coat should have the right to wear it, he would have to produce for himself an amount of useful things equal to 125 francs. It is thus that matters go on all the world over, except that the immense majority of workmen content themselves with a cheaper and more comfortable garment than the black coat supplied by Alfred or Humann. No producer here below is fool enough to believe that, in creating the part, he acquires a right to the whole. This idea could only occur to fishers in troubled waters, personally interested in confounding all notions of what is right.

The worthy poor persons who cut diamonds in a garret have sometimes more thousands of francs lying on their board than five-francs pieces in their drawers. Yet, one would have a bad reception were one to say, "These fine stones, to which you give so much polish, are yours." "No," they would reply, " that which is alone our property is the cutting, the polish which we add to the rough stone. When the diamonds are intrusted to us, they already contain a value which other persons had added in finding them, in transporting them, in assorting them. The merchant does not owe us more than the price of the added value which we ourselves have produced. If our day's work only adds to a diamond, worth two millions, the value of five francs, only five francs are due to us."

To give the equivalent of what we receive, to receive the equivalent of what we give : such is the machinery of exchange.

But by what sign do we recognize that two things are equivalent ? Not much labour is required to prove that a gramme of pure gold is worth another gramme of pure gold; that each of two hectolitres of grain, yielded by the same field, is worth the other. Yet, in the infinite variety of things and of services which men interchange daily, how shall we contrive not to give either more or less than we receive, not to be either rogue or dupe ? A pin set with brilliants, a basket of potatoes, an orchestra stall at the opera, a ride in a cab, a doctor's visit, a pilot's services, the rent of a room, a pair of boots, a forest of a hundred hectares, a mason's day-wage,—these things and services have no relation to each other. How do we know that the one is worth one, or two, or three, or a thousand times more than the other.

There is nothing absolute in value. It is but a relation between the things and services offered and demanded between men. It varies with place, time, the circumstances, wants, and tastes of the contracting parties. Two houses, identical in construction, but situated, the one in Paris, the other in Quimper, are to each other as three is to one. It is necessary to give three in Quimper to get one in Paris. At Paris even, you may see a piece of house property which, without gaining or losing a slate, was worth two in 1846, one in 1848, three in 1868. In the course of twenty years its value has diminished by one-half, and been trebled afterwards.

The relation of wine to grain, in their proportionate value, varies from year to year in the same country. Suppose that two hectolitres of Montpellier wine could be generally exchanged to-day for a hectolitre of grain. A bad vintage might double the value of the wine, and make it to cost as dear as grain ; a bad harvest might produce the contrary effect, and lead to the exchange of four hectolitres of wine for one of grain.

In a city built to shelter 100,000 persons, the population falls to 50,000. Houses are there more offered than they are required, for they are offered to 100,000 persons, and there are only 50,000 to take them. The price of the service rendered by the landlords to the tenants falls at once. But let an occasion attract a crowd of 200,000 persons for three days, and the demand for accommodation will exceed the supply, and the service rendered by the landlord rises.

If 20,000 Parisians are simultaneously struck with the desire to go to a theatre which only holds 1500, the value of places increases in a marvellous proportion; but, on the day when only 50 spectators care to see the piece, the 1500 places, more offered than demanded, fetch nothing.

Suppose that Europe requires each year 1,000,000 bales of cotton. On the day when, by any accident, the supply of this product falls to 500,000 bales, the value of the cotton is doubled, that is to say, twice as much wine, grain, or iron must be given in order to obtain the same quantity of cotton.

By an opposite effect, if the production of cloves were increased tenfold, the consumption remaining the same, their value would fall ninety per cent. This is what occurred on the day when the Imaun of Muscat glutted Europe with this product.

We put aside the value due to affection which could be only appreciated by particular persons, and the exceptional value which is suddenly developed owing to circumstances. A badly-painted family portrait would be worth its weight in gold to Mr A. or Mr B., but it would not fetch two francs at a public sale. There are cases when one would give a kingdom for a horse, or a million for a glass of water. We have seen young simpletons exchange their patrimony for a lock of hair, for which a man of sense would not give anything: social economy does not concern itself with these exceptions.

As a general rule, the more a thing is in demand, the greater is its value. The larger its supply, the less is it worth. And what I say of things applies to services, for things are nothing but consolidated services. Whether a workman gives up to you ten hours of labour, or whether he sells you the product he has made in ten hours, is one and the same.

The economic value of all things and all services is not a mean between Peter's offer and Paul's demand, but between the general supply and the general demand. A starving man or a lunatic might exchange his watch for a morsel of bread; it does not follow by any means that a watch and a morsel of bread are products of equal value. Normal exchange is that which competition has equalized and sanctioned. It operates as follows.

We are all egotists, or, to speak more politely,

6

the instinct of preservation leads each of us to prefer himself to every one else. The tendency of the individual in every exchange is to obtain the utmost that is possible in giving the least that is possible. Do I calumniate humanity? Tell me, honest consumer, if you would hesitate a moment between the baker who should sell you his bread for ten centimes, and him who should give you the same weight and the same quality for a sou? Tell me, honest producer, if the thought would occur to you to sweat for ten sous an hour in front of an establishment where you were offered a franc? What man is fool enough to pay dearly for that which he can buy cheaply? Where are the workmen to be found who are so simple as to give the preference to the smaller offer?

The place of exchange is a hall of continual adjudication where man, whether buyer or seller, runs up his own labour, and runs down the labour of others, and does so without bad faith, for he is naturally disposed to exaggerate the value of all he produces or possesses, to depreciate the value of others' labour and possessions.

However, it is necessary to find a reason for this and to submit to the lessons of experience. If you have a horse to sell, you may well estimate it in your own mind at one hundred thousand francs; after all the possible purchasers have offered you

EXCHANGE. 103

eight, nine, ten thousand francs at the most, you will
end by admitting that its maximum value is ten
thousand francs, and that you must either keep it yourself or exchange it for ten thousand francs. However good an opinion you have of your talents, and
though you are intimately persuaded that your
labour is worth more than one hundred francs the
hour, you must work for four francs a day, or fold
your hands, if no one offers you higher pay. You
belong to a country where the kilo of cherries is
worth thirty centimes in June; when in St Peters-
burg, where all the greengrocers sell them for six
roubles, where all the buyers pay six roubles, you
must necessarily go without cherries, or admit that
cherries in June are worth six roubles at St Peters-
burg. You are accustomed to pay forty centimes
the hour to your workmen. If they refuse to work
for less than fifty centimes, and if you cannot find
others to do the work at the old rate, you are obliged
to admit that their hour is worth fifty centimes;
labour must be recompensed at its value, or you
must deprive yourself of their services.

The machinery of exchange does not work without jolts; it may even happen that an imprudent
person may have his fingers caught in the gearing.
But, as we all stand in need of each other, we necessarily end by coming to an understanding. The

producer's interest is to give his services for the price offered ; the consumer's interest is to approximate to the price asked, under the penalty, in both cases, of foregoing the profit on the exchange.

Now, what is admirable in exchange is that it benefits the two contracting parties in almost equal measure. Each of the two, by giving what he has for that which he has not, makes a good bargain.

It appears surprising, at first sight, that two persons can simultaneously gain the one by the other. This is, however, what occurs at every free and straightforward exchange. When a broker brings a buyer and seller together, he asks a commission from each, which both pay without question : this proves they think that they have both gained by the ex- change.·

In fact, whether you sell, whether you buy, you perform an act of preference. No one constrains you to give over any of your things for the things of another. You yourself prefer to give what you have in excess, for that in which you are deficient. Even should you not have anything in excess, were you one of those unfortunates whom a pitiless necessity reduces to exchange the counterpane of their bed for a few days' bread, you still realize a profit, because you hand over an object of secondary importance for an article of primary importance. If your counterpane were actually more useful than the bread, you would not consent to the exchange. . You perform it, therefore you acknowledge it is advantageous for you at the moment.

When you enter a shop in order to procure half a kilo of candles for six grammes of a white metal, you instinctively thank the person who hands you the candles, and he thanks you in turn when you hand him your money. You are right, and the seller is so too, because you have been exchanging service for service with another man, your equal. He has given you a thing more useful for your purpose than money. If you had kept your money in your pocket, if the exchange of one thing for another had been denied you, nothing would prevent you from breaking your nose against the furniture on returning home; you would not be able to read the book lying on your night-table by the light of your money.

In handing over his light in sticks, the retailer, that humble producer, has also done a good stroke of business. He did not acquire his merchandise for the purpose of consumption, but in order to sell it; he owes the price of it to the wholesale dealer, whom he must pay in money on the appointed day. You have helped him to fulfil a sacred engagement, to liquidate an anterior exchange. You give him in addition a few centimes as the price of the personal service he has rendered you. And what service? Are you unaware of it? Is it nothing to have transported, preserved, divided for your use and put within reach of your hand, a useful thing which you had neither the time nor, perchance, the means of getting from the manufactory in quantities of a hundred kilos.

If men would but reason a little, they would all be in a state of admiration and gratitude in presence of the beneficent mechanism of exchange. It permits us to obtain all the things we want, all the services which we should not be able to render to ourselves. And at what price? Through performing useful labour, it matters not what, this being always left to our choice.

Perhaps you have not inquired by what combination a working locksmith, for instance, manufactures his bread, his wine, his meat, his clothes, his lodging, the education of his children, and all useful things, by strokes of file and hammer.

He has not inherited a centiare of land; he cannot plough, reap, grind, or bake, and yet he eats bread. He has never harvested grapes in his life, and he restores his strength by drinking wine. He has never reared a head of cattle, and he eats meat and he wears shoes. He cannot spin, weave, or stitch, and he has linen and clothes. Two powerful horses, which he does not feed, draw him to his work-room, if at a distance, and bring him back. He has never dreamed about building a house, and is well or ill lodged. His arms are the only arms he has at his disposal, and he lives in full security: he does not fear either the evil-doers of his country or European armies of which the effective strength is from two to three millions of men. He has his judges, his police; he has an army always ready to fight on his behalf.

What has he done to-day, from eight in the morning to six in the evening, to pay his quota for so many things and for so many services?

He has hung up bells.

Is it not wonderful? But the finest part of the matter is that the workman in question is not indebted to a soul; this is because he owes nothing, at the close of the account, to those who have clothed, fed, housed, carried, and protected him. He has given an equivalent for all that he has received; he has exchanged his services for the services of others. Doubtless, he owes a certain acknowledgment to his contemporaries whose labour simplifies and lightens his life, but his contemporaries owe him quite as much, through reciprocity. And the balance will always remain even, so long as he pays for what he buys, and produces the equivalent of what he consumes.

We are all dependent upon each other, because

our wants are always more varied than our aptitudes.

Let us lay this truth to heart, and we shall be the more just towards each other, and comprehend that the first exchange to be made between men is an exchange of good sentiments and of good offices.

Each of us buys, sells, and re-sells, and it may be said that, in general, equity presides over all our exchanges. But the science of economic laws is so little diffused that no one submits to the laws of the market without slightly protesting. We make use of each other while murmuring against each other. Were it fully demonstrated to us that our things or our services were paid for at the *current rate*, we should still call out "Thief!" because we exaggerate the value of what we give and underrate the things we receive.

The earth does not revolve once round its axis without your hearing some complaints of lenders against borrowers, of borrowers against lenders, of consumers against merchants, of merchants against manufacturers, of manufacturers against workmen, of workmen against their masters. What is consumed collectively is as fertile in misunderstanding as what is consumed privately: the public complains that its servants are too well paid, while the servants complain of not being paid according to merit; in fine,

one half of the human race spends its life in recrimin-
ations against the other half.

The truth is that the lender renders a service to
the borrower in making over to him the enjoyment
of a useful thing, while the borrower renders an
equivalent service to the lender in restoring to him,
for instance, 105 francs in place of the 100 he had
received. If these two kinds of benefits were not
generally recognized as mutual, the lenders would
long refuse to lend or the borrowers would long refuse to borrow. Traders render a service to consumers in procuring merchandise for them; the consumer renders a service to the trader in paying him
higher for his merchandise than he would do at the
manufactory. The contractor renders a service to
his workmen in assuring them the regular employment of their faculties, in lending them tools which
are often costly, in emancipating them from the tur-
moil of a sale, in securing them against the risks of
commerce. Workmen render a service to the contractor in selling him for ten sous a service which
he sometimes disposes of for a franc. Public servants
render a service to the people in transacting their
business: the people render them a service in asking
them to sign a receipt monthly.

If you think that your services are not recompensed
at what they are worth, you have always the right

to sell them to the highest bidder. If you find that a service is sold to you too dearly, you are at liberty to beat it down, or to perform it yourself, or to dispense with it, if not unavoidable.

Let each one procure the necessaries of life at the price he can; let us bargain as much as we please; nothing can be more just. But, in the name of Heaven, let us give up the deplorable habit of believing that we are imposed upon by those who serve us, and of treating them as inferiors.

When Peter buys his sugar and his coffee from Paul, he thinks himself on that account his superior. "He is my tradesman!" Be it so, he is your purveyor of Colonial wares, but you are his purveyor of gold and silver. Gold and silver are Colonial wares also. The shop is right in thinking that it keeps the factory going; the manufacturer rightly regards the trader as being indebted to him: the contractor says that he supports his work-people; that is true; the work-people cry that they support the contractors; that is correct. The domestic, in speaking of his master, says, "A man whom I have served for ten years." The master, in speaking of his servant, replies, "A fellow whom I have lodged, boarded, and clothed during ten years." Neither the one nor the other says what is untrue, but they do wrong in forgetting that they have received an equivalent for their services and in treating him who has paid them as their debtor.

The exchange of equal quantities cannot become a source of inequality.

By rights we are all equal, that is to say, the human personality, as far as it extends, is everywhere equally sacred and inviolable.

We are unequal in strength, in intelligence, in virtue, in activity, in wealth. One produces more, another less, according to age, aptitude, determination, and tools. But as exchange applies only to services which are equivalents, it cannot subordinate one producer to another. The million says to the franc: give me a sou and I will return you five centimes. In consequence of this operation, the million and the franc preserve their respective positions: the million would be an idiot if it thought itself the benefactor of the franc; the franc would be a fool if it thought itself imposed upon by the million.

Thus exchange does not heighten the inequality of fortune, which is the torment of the envious. But neither has it the effect of levelling riches. It profits rich and poor in equal proportions, by permitting each to choose the most useful or the most agreeable thing. What tends to level human conditions are the indolence and the prodigality of those having possessions, the labour and saving of those who wish to acquire possessions.

If the dogma of human interdependence required to be proved, the mechanism of exchange would furnish a striking demonstration. Supply causes a fall in price, that is, all useful things are cheaper the more plentiful they are. Should the quantity of food, dwellings, clothing, of useful things, be doubled throughout the world, we should procure in five hours of labour what we now obtain in ten. If the total amount of useful things were reduced by one half, it would be necessary to work twenty hours for what now takes ten. This is no mere hypothesis, but a truth proved by experience.

Are all men, without exception, interested in acquiring all things cheaply, that is to say, in getting the utmost possible amount of things in exchange for the smallest amount of labour? Yes. Therefore all men have an equal interest in hindering destruction, in countenancing production and saving.

The destruction of anything whatsoever, directly affects its possessor and indirectly all other men. The burning of one quarter raises the rents in a whole city; demolish the fourth of the houses upon earth and all rents would rise one-fourth. Destroy the half of the grain harvest and bread will be twice as dear next year. Stop the production of cotton in

some American States and the Parisian joiners will
pay more for their shirts. When a dock or a great
warehouse is destroyed anywhere, at London or at
Bordeaux, with the merchandise stored in it, the
provision for the human race is diminished by so
much, and the loss is distributed over all men. Pil-
lage and robbery, we have already said, are equivalent to the destruction of property. This is why
each of us is led by a natural impulse to put out
fires, to repress crimes, to battle energetically with
all the plagues which threaten the property of our
fellows. This is why instinct, anterior to reasoning,
saddens you at the news of a war or a shipwreck.

Great epidemics, as well as wars and ship-
wrecks, carry off a multitude of able-bodied persons,
capable of reimbursing the human community the
advances made to them. Thus, if you reason, your
heart will be rent every time you are told of the
destruction of men. Egotists will say, " What does
the cholera matter to me, seeing it is in India?
What do I care for civil war, if it is waged by
Americans? The Taepings have cut the throats of
the population of a province, but I think nothing of
that ; it happened in China." The following would be
your reply to these unhappy persons blinded by their
misunderstood interest, " Neither the distances which
separate us, nor the diversities of origin, of colour,

and of civilization which distinguish us, nor even the misunderstandings which sometimes array us in arms against each other, hinder humanity from forming a great body. The sum of useful things produced in a year on the surface of the globe constitutes the collective receipts of the human race; the sum of the products there consumed represents its outlay; the total savings which are realized in a year is added to the common capital and makes humanity wealthier. The richer the great community of men becomes, the more useful things will the individual procure in exchange for his daily labour. Thus the simple workman who files and polishes metal in a Parisian garret is interested in the utmost possible quantity of silk being produced in China, the utmost possible quantity of wool in Australia, the utmost possible quantity of iron in Sweden, and in the small possible quantity of things being destroyed in these places: for the more that useful things abound here below, the better your labour and mine will be remunerated by exchange."

Now, all useful things are the product of man, and of adult man. The day on which one hundred thousand adults fall in the field of battle, there are one hundred thousand producers the less, and the collective production of humanity decreases in proportion. I know that this great blank will soon be filled up by fresh births, but one hundred thousand new-born babes do not replace one hundred thousand grown-up men. Twenty years will elapse before they are good for anything, and, during these twenty years, the community of the human race to which we belong will have to support them on credit. The destruction of one hundred thousand men is thus a real loss, which is spread over the whole human race, the conqueror in this great battle not excepted. He has obtained the advantages he most desires for the time being. But quarrels are simply an accident in the life of humanity; the most important political questions have their day; the economic interest which renders all of us interdependent is eternal and unchangeable. Two nations go to war to-day, yet they prepare their samples for exchange in the great exhibition of to-morrow.

I should think myself doing insult to my readers were I to insist at greater length on this point, but, unfortunately, it is not useless to demonstrate to my contemporaries two other truths equally certain. The first is, that all men, without exception, have a personal interest in instructing other men. The second is that all men, without exception, are personally interested in enriching other men.

I emphatically declare, in the teeth of the worthless rich (if any remain), and of the wicked poor (if there be any), that human interdependence extends as far as that. Our destinies are so closely entwined by the bonds of exchange. Neither the rich nor the poor practise injustice for its own sake. But, just as each body of the state is subject to a professional malady, so is each large class of society liable to special prejudices.

Now, the poor and the rich have always had courtiers who confirmed them in error instead of dragging them out of it; who set them at loggerheads, instead of preaching peace and concord. For once that the rich hear it said, " It is your interest to enrich and enlighten the poor," they are told twenty times in all strains, " Do not listen to those who banter on the plea of serving you. Every one for himself. You are wealthy, instructed; thanks to God, you occupy a high position; you soar to the extent of 200,000 francs got from the funds, above those who have nothing. For what purpose should you personally annihilate the distance which makes your greatness ? I grant that it would not cost you anything; that you could adorn the mind of Paul and give a pension to Peter without depriving yourself of a centime. You would no longer be what you were relatively to these fellows. They would pretend to be on an equality with you; you would have

manufactured equals, and who then would clean
your boots? Society, when stable, rests on an inequality of conditions. The poor are indispensable,
were it only to serve the rich, and the poor are
tractable only when their poverty is doubled by
ignorance. When all men shall be able to read,
there will no longer be a quarter of an hour's
stability in the affairs of this world."

The unfortunate, who, alas, are in a great majority on the earth, do not require to be taught to
detest the rich man's millions. Too honest to break
open his strong box, they experience a sort of agreeable tingling at the news that a scoundrel has forced
it open. They will not set his house on fire, they
will even go to extinguish the flames at the risk of their
lives; but if you relate to them that a certain mansion is reduced to ashes, that a certain safe filled with
gold or diamonds has disappeared in the hubbub,
you will find them more ready to laugh than to cry
over the occurrence. At whatever page we open
history, we meet with an ignorant and suffering multitude which does not dread public disasters, which
rather longs for them, just as the invalid, fatigued with
being in bed, calls for the quack's poisons and knives,
and which finds a sort of desperate consolation in
dreaming about the demolition of the social edifice.

In every country, in every age, these unfortunates have had interested courtiers who told them, "Destroy everything ; you have nothing to lose."

Poor people ! You have everything to lose which other men possess around you. Your present condition is hard enough, I admit; it would be unbearable, if some catastrophe deprived you of that which is not your own. All the abundance of things which saving has accumulated in other hands is not in your possession, for the time being, but it is at your disposal, at your service, within your reach. Does this imply that you have but to stretch forth your hand to draw upon the common treasure ? Not exactly, but it suffices to employ a rather more complicated gesture. Stir your arms, my friends, and exchange will permit you to draw upon all the treasures of the earth, upon the granaries of the farmer, upon the cellars of the wine-grower, upon the stores of the manufacturer, upon the coffers of the banker. Fortunate poor, indeed, you can choose out of all the riches of this world, on condition of furnishing an equivalent in labour.

Rejoice, then, to witness around you an enormous accumulation of useful things, because the more of them there are the less they will cost, and thank fortune for having cast your lot in a wealthy age and country. Return thanks to the innumerable generations of laborious and economic producers who have left so many fine and excellent things behind them. Five hundred years ago, in a century less fortunate than that in which you live, you would have had to labour four days for what now costs ten hours of toil. A thousand leagues off, in a certain country poorer than France, man has to make an effort four times greater in order to obtain less than you do.

I commend this reasoning to the consideration of the working classes, that is to say, of those who, like myself, have brought no other capital into the world than their head and their arms. And, as this is a grave matter, I do not think I err in dwelling upon it for a little.

Each of us, in order to live, requires to obtain two kinds of services; firstly, real, contemporary, so to speak, simultaneous services: the baker, while kneading his dough, requires a wine-grower to harvest wine for him, a tailor to stitch his clothes, a washerwoman to wash his shirts. These diverse services are reciprocally exchanged among living persons. But human life, in a civilized country, requires services of another nature, whereof the source ascends far beyond our birth, which might be called the benefits of the dead. If you reflect for two minutes only, you will recognize that at the moment of your birth there were here below houses built, furniture, implements, reclaimed land, wrought metals, furnishings of every kind, — in a word, riches produced by labour, and that the authors of these things were nearly all dead before you were thought of. It may be said, without exaggeration, that the largest portion of existing riches is a bequest of the dead. The whole of these substantial things forms the capital of the human race. It consists of all which men have saved since the beginning of time; in other words, of all which humanity has produced without consuming.

But these bequests of the dead belong to their heirs, and the working man is not the heir of anybody. How shall he obtain a share of these riches, without which he cannot live? By exchanging a part of his actual labour for a fraction of consolidated labour. Out of the ten hours he spends in the workshop, there are six or seven which will be exchanged, without his noticing it, for the time and labour of other working men, his contemporaries, who are toiling for him whilst he is toiling for them. The remainder is set apart to pay for the enjoyment or the possession of the durable things which existed on the earth before him; the rent of his house, his furniture, his tools, the interest on the small sums he borrows, &c.

On the other hand, the heir of the dead, landlord

or capitalist, performs an inverse operation : he exchanges a part of his consolidated things for a certain quantity of actual labour. What does he do when paying his servants' wages? He gives a portion of capital, or of old labour, for the equivalent amount of their labour. When he gives employment, when he sends his housekeeper to market, when he buys a pair of horses, the act is always the same; he exchanges a product of olden date for more recent products with which he cannot dispense.

Thus the holders of capital are absolutely in want of the working man's labour, just as the working man, in order to lodge himself, to procure tools, to live, stands in need of capital.

It is unfortunately certain that if capitalists were allowed to regulate the conditions of exchange by themselves, they would so contrive as to get much while giving little. Not less certain is it that if working men could arbitrarily fix the tariff of their services, they would cause themselves to be paid as dearly as possible ; but supply and demand interpose to balance these reciprocal claims.

Now we have admitted, on the strength of experience, that supply necessarily leads to a fall in prices, and that the more abundant merchandise becomes, the more of it can be procured cheaply. Thus it is evident that the more capital, or consolidated property,

there is in the world, the working man will be able
to get more of it cheaply, or obtain high wages,
which is the same thing.

Working men are interested in their handiwork
being bid for by competing capitalists. It is at this
price that they arrive at obtaining not only necessaries, but superfluities, and at becoming capitalists
in turn, if they are prudent, for the savings of the
present form the capital of the future.

Hence, instead of railing against the fortune of
others, the working man ought to wish for as many
rich men as possible. This must be demonstrated.

As for you, rich men, you would do the most foolish thing in the world, if you should dream of perpetuating the poverty and ignorance of others. Are you
unaware that poverty and ignorance condemn the
healthiest and most robust individual to a sort of
quasi-sterility? That the more one knows, the
more one is able to produce? That good intentions
being equal, an educated working man renders ten
times more services than an ignorant one? That
tools, namely, the beginning of riches, often increase
the quantity of useful labour tenfold and a hundred-
fold? That actual, contemporary labour, with which
you cannot dispense, will cost you so much the less
the more it is offered, will be the more offered the
more easy it is, and will be all the easier the better

it is enlightened or equipped ? I add, merely that it may be borne in mind, a consideration which has its value, namely, that the security of your persons and property will constantly increase in proportion to the degree of public well-being and education. Will you now deny that self-interest, rightly understood, impels you to instruct and enrich those who are destitute ?

Hence the poor man ought to wish for the opulence of the rich, and do so in his own interest.

The rich ought to wish the poor to be well off, and do so out of pure selfishness.

And social economy ascends to such a height that it merges into universal morality. For man's reason is indivisible, and there are no truths which cannot be reconciled with each other. What would happen if the poor, out of calculation, were to apply themselves to enrich the rich ? If the rich, out of a wise selfishness, were to apply themselves to enrich the poor ? Who would be the gainer in such an event ? Everybody.

The area we inhabit is limited, but the production of useful things is unlimited. Oh ! how fine would be the victories and how vast the conquests if, instead of fighting against each other, we were to unite all our efforts against blind and stupid nothingness !

CHAPTER VI.

WE have seen wise economy join hands with morality and countersign, after her, the law of interdependence.

Yesterday she said to you, " All men are brethren." She comes and tells you to-day, "All men are free. Free to work when and how they please, to produce, to consume, to exchange, at the price agreed upon, things and services of every kind." This follows from the very definition of law. In principle, the individual rightfully does what he pleases, provided he harms nobody. His right has no other limit than the right of another. The sole barrier which stops him is the inviolability of other men, respected and sacred by the same title as his own.

It is natural, therefore, that I should select from among useful labours the one that suits my faculties the best ; that I should produce the things I prefer to produce, that I should consume what I like of them, and that I should exchange the surplus, when in the humour, for the things which appear to me preferable. This deduction is so logical that one is almost ashamed to put it in writing for the instruction of an enlightened people.

But in the moral as in the physical order of things there are mines as old as the world and discovered only yesterday. Gold lay long dormant in the Californian placers before it dazzled Europe and America; the true notion of right long slumbered in the depths of the conscience before enlightening the human race. Think, moreover, that, from the beginning of ages to our day, when we discuss this great question in concert, there have been slaves here below! Slaves, that is, men who do not belong to themselves, and who are like the hands, the arms, and the feet of another head. The first time that a conqueror, through satiety or through fatigue, would neither eat nor despatch his victim, he said to him, "I grant you life on condition that you live for me. Your labour belongs to me; all that you produce will be mine, your children included, if I should allow you to cohabit. Enter this stable for men and wait there for your companions." Think that this noble France, in which we account it an honour to be born, did not abolish slavery throughout its length and

7

breadth till 1789 and slavery in its colonies till 1848. Recall to mind that slavery is still a flourishing institution in four out of five quarters of the globe, and is maintained in a corner of the fifth.

The slave's production is arbitrarily determined by his master. It is his master who says to him, "You must cultivate this piece of land," or, "You must work a mill," or, "You must educate my sons." The slave's consumption is regulated by his master: "Here are your clothes for the year and your rations for the day." Of exchange, between master and slave, there is no question. The one owes nothing; the other owes everything.

Between absolute slavery and absolute liberty occurs an intermediate form, tutelage. The free population of France remained in tutelage up to 1789. If you analyze in good faith and without carping, the principle of our ancient monarchy, this is what you gather from it: the king, delegated by Heaven to the government over a great people and over a vast territory, ought to represent Providence here below by securing, if possible, the happiness of his subjects. His absolute power is but an instrument which he employs for the profit of some millions of men; or, to speak more correctly, of infants, since all the French are minors in relation to him. As a father does in the case of his sons, so does he prohibit his subjects from indulging in what he considers exaggerated expenses. He publishes edicts against luxury at table, in carriages, or in clothes. Sumptuary laws, designed to limit each one's consumption, succeed each other from Charlemagne up to the last days of Louis XIV. And Diderot's *Encyclopædia*, the most daring monument of the French mind prior to 1789, innocently desires that these laws should be put in force.

A good father warns his children against the danger of reading bad books. The king reads all books before his people, and allows only the good to be printed, or those he considers good.

Paternal authority assigns a career to each of the children. The king allows certain persons to follow professions from which he excludes others. He reserves some for himself; he decides that a particular industry shall flourish at a particular place, in certain hands, and that no one shall meddle therein without permission. Each trading body is organized under the shelter of a good and solid monopoly; trade tends to become hereditary, as in Egypt, according to the ideal set forth by Bossuet in his discourse to the great Dauphin: "The law assigns to each one his profession, which is handed down from father to son. One must neither exercise two professions nor change the profession; one does best that which one has seen others do, in which one has been solely trained from infancy."

The noblest spirit of the old rule, even when launching into Utopian speculations, went no further than an improved tutelage. Witness Fénelon in his imaginary monarchy of Salente. He fixes the quantity of land which each family may possess; he imposes an official plan upon all private dwellings; he determines the clothing of all the citizens according to their rank; he draws up the bill of fare for each meal, limits the quantity of wine which they may drink, prohibits the consumption of liquors, of perfumes, of rich embroideries, of figured stuffs, of jewellery, of effeminate music; he regulates the furniture of each family, plucks up half of the vines in the country, takes all the workmen employed in articles of luxury and sends them into the fields, decrees fines and even imprisonment against those among the poor who cultivate their land badly, establishes "magistrates to whom traders render an account of their effects, of their gains, of their expenses, and of their undertakings. They were never permitted to risk the things of others, and they could not risk more than the half of their own. In other respects commerce was entirely free." What is your opinion?

It is not without design that I have cited two books written under the eyes of the great king, by two royal preceptors, for the instruction of the heirs to the throne.

Royalty by Divine Right thought it did well in meddling with all things; it imitated to the extent of its humble means the Providence on high which watches over everything, down to the smallest things of the world. The sovereign acted in good faith when he conferred monopolies upon nearly every industry, when he determined the conditions of capacity, of morality, of means, without which no one could be a jeweller, cabinet-maker, or draper.

Whilst a certain number of citizens were excluded from industry on account of their inferiority, others were kept away from it on account of their nobility. A gentleman could neither work with his hands, nor trade in a small way, without losing caste. The king thought then, as did nearly all the people, that idleness was more honourable to man than hard or grinding labour. The king sincerely thought he was protecting his subjects by prohibiting the exportation of a particular product and permitting the importation of another. Even up to the time of Colbert numbers of interior custom-houses were maintained, and these hindered the people of one province from exchanging their products with other Frenchmen, their neighbours. It was believed that all this contributed to the utmost prosperity of the people.

Authorized producers did not hesitate to prefer their monopoly to the general good; but they were neither very happy nor very free. By granting privileges, the monarchy had, so to speak, doubled its responsibility; it knew this, and acted accordingly. The sentiment of its duty led it to regulate everything, to supervise everything, to control all products. A piece of cloth did not leave the factory, any more than a volume the printing-press, without the stamp and guaranty of the government.

Logic compelled our kings to carry such a system to its extreme consequences. A father ought not to allow his children to treat each other like negroes and obtain too great a superiority the one over the other. It was necessary, then, to intervene between the buyer and the seller, between the lender and the borrower, between the master and the workman, not only to hinder fraud, but to limit the profits of each. Hence these laws relating to the maximum which traverse our entire history, and of which some, in virtue of an acquired speed, have continued to our day. To cite but one of them, the legal rate of interest was about 8 per cent. up to 1602, about 6 per cent. up to 1634, from $5\frac{1}{2}$ up to 1665, when the king fixed it at 5. An edict reduced it to 2 per cent. in 1730, but without effect; in 1734 it was $3\frac{1}{3}$, and rose to 5 in the following year. But the rate of interest was not the same in all the

provinces of the kingdom; the parliaments sometimes refused to register the edicts, and besides, the
laws of supply and demand had always more authority than the absolute power of the king.

I put on one side all the injustices of the ancient
regime, the arbitrary division of imposts, the inequality of men elevated into a principle and corrupting all contracts, the labouring class utilized for
the profit of a handful of idlers, the tribute levied
by the rich upon the labour of the poor, the tithes,
the enforced labour, the socage tenure, the ban, the
field-rent, without prejudice to the reasonable tax
which the citizen ought always to pay to the State. I
regard in this organization only the effects of royal
tutelage and the injury done to good intentions.
The good will of the kings was not doubtful; they
had a direct interest in making the fortunes of their
people. It was for this end that they regulated everything, labour, rest, culture, industry, seed-time,
harvest, production, and commerce, substituting their
alleged wisdom for the alleged incapacity of the
citizens. Social order appeared to be founded on the
principle that man, when left to himself, is incapable of
acting properly. The whole people walked in leading-
strings, like a big child, directed by the king, and
the prudence of the rulers combined with the patience
of the governed conducted us straightway to ruin.

We have all heard it stated that the Revolution of 1789 had substituted liberty for tutelage. Who among us has not felt his heart beat at the story of the admirable night of the 4th of August? For my part, I know of nothing finer than that hecatomb of privileges and abuses spontaneously immolated by the privileged orders themselves.

But if you read history a little more closely, the revolutionary period, despite its grandeur and its glory, will appear to you as a general suspension of every liberty. It seems that the sun had appeared an instant, only to be immediately eclipsed. The account of these ten years, which Europe regards with envy, may be thus stated: devotion, patriotism, civil and military courage, unlimited; political and economic liberties, nil.

I state this without accusing anybody. Political liberty is impossible at the period of a revolution. Each one pursues his ideal of government and sees conspirators in all those who do not think exactly as he does. Hence hatred, revenge, and measures of public safety.

Economic liberties are no less incompatible with uncertainty and agitation in the public mind. During the absence of stable and unquestioned laws, each one fears not only to be enslaved, but to be robbed or starved. In all the popular movements of our great

revolution the leaders have been governed by a
political idea, true or false, while the mass of the
people have thought to solve a problem of social economy, the question of bread.

Hardly had the Bastille been demolished than the
people of Paris cut the throats of Foulon and Berthier.
For what crime? Because bread was dear; these
unfortunate men were accused of forestalling corn.
On the 5th of October, Paris threw itself upon Ver-
sailles and forced Louis XVI. to occupy the Tuileries:
it was supposed that his presence would lower the
price of bread. As plenty did not arrive the bakers
were attacked, and the unfortunate François was
hanged from a lamp-post.

When the weak become strong, when the op-
pressed become free, their first impulse is not to use,
but to abuse, their opportunities. Unshackle the
hands of a worthy man bound without legitimate
reason: he will not cast away the chain, but will
carefully pick it up in order to fetter the hands of
him by whom he was manacled. Were he to act
otherwise, he would not be a man but an angel.
This is why the ignorant masses, who then formed
the majority of the French people, extemporized a
social economy for their use and benefit. The poor
man had been actually turned to account by the
privileged classes: he did not in any wise content

himself with helping to suppress abuses, but he desired to turn the tables on the rich, as the conqueror turns against his foe the pieces of cannon he has captured from him. The history of revolutionary spoliations is too well known to require me to narrate it. But one does not halt on the slope of arbitrary acts : the poor man went on to despoil the poor man, wherever he felt himself the stronger. For example, the buyers said one fine morning, in the market of Etampes, " Corn has been always assessed to our loss ; to-day, by our own authority, we will assess it to our profit." This was robbing the farmer, who, indeed, was not rich in 1791.

The Mayor of the town ventured to defend commercial freedom and sound political economy ; he was murdered in the market. About the same time, in Paris, the Faubourgs thought fit to assess groceries after their fashion, and all the small tradesmen were ruined in a day. But those acts of violence, though unpunished by the Legislative Assembly, had no legal character. Two years later the Convention legally organized the ruin of all commerce by the laws about forestalling and the maximum. To be a forestaller of any kind was to withdraw wares of primary importance from circulation,—grain, flour, bread, wine, meat, eatables, iron, leather, cloth, stuffs. Whoever possessed a certain quantity of them was bound, under pain of death, to put them on sale, in retail quantities, and the authorities fixed the maximum price of everything. And one became a forestaller on easy terms, for the Girondin Valazé, in his report to the Convention, denounced Louis XVI. as being a forestaller of corn, of sugar, and of coffee. Poor man! The newspapers had reproached him with the peaches he ate during the sitting of the 8th of August.

From the point of view of commercial freedom, forestalling is neither a crime nor a misdemeanour, but it is often a piece of folly which costs its author dear. If any Parisian were to think fit now to buy up all the disposable grain in the market with the view of re-selling it at a rise next month, the mere announcement of a deficiency would make all the agriculturists of the vicinity rush to Paris with millions of hectolitres. It is necessary that the forestaller should buy all that is offered, or renounce any profit from his speculation. And, when he had bought all the harvests of the vicinity, all the neighbouring departments would hasten to the market, and, if he did not purchase everything again, he would see grain flow in from the East and the West, from the North and the South, from Corsica and Algeria. And were he rich enough to obtain possession of all the national reserves, Germany, Belgium, England, Spain, Italy, Egypt, and Southern Russia would discharge their products in the market-place, and the imprudent speculator for a rise would only reap a fall.

Corn was dear during all the Revolution; the whole of France suffered from scarcity, the Parisians excepted, who, owing to an entirely despotic privilege, were fed at the nation's expense. Bread was *given* to them at the price of three sous the pound, three sous in assignats! Now, there was a time when three sous in assignats were not worth the hundredth part of a silver centime, as 2000 francs in paper represented 15 sous. The country gave more than 90 millions in silver each year, in order to procure this small gratification to the inhabitants of Paris. Everywhere else, the necessaries of life were unprocurable for money, and the people were at their wits' end what to do. The people are always in the same trouble when they make a revolution, for revolutions inevitably bring about scarcity, and search as they will, they never lay hands upon the real forestallers.

Alas, the unique cause of this dearness is the revolution itself. It dries up public prosperity at the fountain-head. Cheapness can only spring from plenty. Plenty can only proceed from labour. And there is no labour where security is absent, no security without the regular movement of national laws and institutions.

The poor citizens of Paris obtained a fee of two francs, in silver, when they attended the meetings of their sections, and the sections met together twice a week. These four francs were not only a ridiculous subsidy; they constituted a heavy burden levied on the labour of the provinces in order to hinder labour in Paris.

All the governments which succeeded have exhibited to us a uniform spectacle. Authority has always been seriously occupied in covering with its tutelary care the economic interests of the citizens, and an Opposition, aiming at overthrowing Authority, has always promised another system of tutelage. Existing authority has protected, or fancied that it has protected, those who have possessions; the aspirants for power have promised their protection to those who have nothing. An old field of battle, and always barren, despite the blood with which we have sprinkled it.

Socialism, which can be discussed to-day without heat, delivered its last stroke before our eyes in June, 1848. It is not only conquered, but is disarmed, owing to the progress of enlightenment and the better state of the public mind. Among those who toil and suffer in French society, a thousand men cannot be found who are so ignorant of their own interest as to seek alleviation in disorder and violence. The problem of universal well-being is not yet solved, I admit, but it is sensibly put, and that is a great point.

It is important that workmen have learned to be on their guard against the charlatans of political economy, those sellers of the philosopher's stone who promise to double our riches by arresting the labour which produces them. It is important that the attempts despotically made to organize labour have miscarried before the eyes of the crowd, and that those who have inherited nothing comprehend that their salvation can only be found in liberty. It is important that a new power, sprung from the nation, and directly interested in procuring the happiness of the greatest number, has had the sense to abandon in principle the system of tutelage, which has given proofs of its incapacity.

You poor who would become rich (and you are right), ask but one thing from Heaven, the liberty peaceably to produce and save. The workman was to be pitied under Louis XIV., but he was still more miserable under Marat, and I dare not think of what he would have underwent under the frightful tutelage of Babeuf.

Proudhon has somewhere said, "Every socialistic sect, from Licurgus to M. Cabet, governs by author-

ity." And Proudhon himself would have required
an authority more sovereign still than that of Louis
XIV., to impose on the French people his pleasant
utopia; the suppression of money, payment of taxes
in kind, confusion of legislative and executive power,
abolition of judicial power, gratuitous loans, confiscation of net incomes, equality of fortunes, re-
establishment of guilds, &c., &c. The beginning of
Proudhon's wisdom is an arbitrary definition, that is,
a despotic one, of value. Value, in our opinion,
is the relation freely settled between two things and
two kinds of service. According to the polemist of
Besançon, value is the price of the return. The
workman makes over to the consumer the product of
his day's labour, reckons his expenses, and says, "I
have eaten so much, drunk so much, my day's rent is
so much; the cost of raw material and the interest on my tools are so much; the expenses of my
family so much; I have laid by for the future, so much;
my assurance against dull times and the accidents of
life, so much. Add up the whole, and you will get
the exact figure of the wage due to me." Happily for
them, the producers who are Proudhon's disciples
have never attempted to rate their services in this
way. Ordinary good sense told them that such a
claim would have put to flight consumers and contractors, and constituted to their prejudice a perpetual

suspension of work. They have modestly accepted the tariffs fixed by supply and demand, that is to say, the laws flowing from the nature of things, and I maintain that they have not done badly.

Shall I say that everything is for the best in our social economy? No; but in recent times we have initiated a pacific revolution, which will end sooner or later in the emancipation of all active forces. And the liberty of production and of exchange will lead to an abundance of things such as our centuries of tutelage have never known or even imagined. The end is still far enough off, and is separated from us by obstacles a century old; but it may be seen, and people and power, the one following the other, are moving towards it by a common effort. For the first time during a long period, power has been the first to act properly; the nation, hesitating at first and almost surprised, marches after and doubles its pace.

What imparts the greatest interest to the times in which we live, and what will do honour to them in history, is the conduct of certain statesmen who one fine morning abjured the most venerable and inveterate errors. We have seen economic truth, confined during half a century in the study of a few thinkers, fly at a single bound as far as the throne.

Monarchy by Divine Right, in its last years, had foreseen and all but adopted the great idea which we proclaim to-day; but no one, not even Turgot, could establish it. A power which has no other reason for its existence than the fact that it exists, is upheld, willingly or not, on what is raised around it. Facts, rights, truths, errors, all combine to form its casual solidity; it perceives standing ground in everything environing it; it dares not touch anything through fear of shaking, by a false move, one of its supports. The sole government which can bring the best accredited errors to the test, is that which cannot itself be called in question because its legitimacy is founded on universal suffrage.

Nearly always, nearly everywhere, the decisions of power more or less retard public opinion. In existing circumstances, we have seen the Tuileries clock decidedly faster than the country. It is certain that several changes wrought in social economy before our eyes have surprised many citizens, and for a moment disquieted certain persons as to their interests.

This is because we have been born in the midst of a state of things which is factitious and illogical, and in many respects iniquitous. A man with good sense, without prejudices of education, without preconceived ideas, who arrives at the head of affairs, must be struck with this economic confusion, and note each anomaly while saying to himself, Why?

Why should consumers, that is, all men, be condemned to pay dearly for a bad or mediocre product when, by crossing the frontier, they can have a better one at a low price?

Why should the producer of corn be obliged to sell his harvest at a low rate on this side of the frontier, when the foreigner offers him a higher price for it on the other side?

Why should the Parisian be free to open a grocer's shop, and should not have the right to become a baker, butcher, cab-driver, broker, publisher, printer, manager of public entertainments? Is there any logical reason why certain kinds of production should be open to every one, and certain others restricted to those who are privileged?

Why should judges, who dispose of the lives, honour, and the liberty of men, gratuitously obtain that quasi-sovereign authority without giving other guarantees than those of talent and virtue, whilst ministerial officers buy for hard cash the right to exercise their industry?

Why, in a country of equality, should masters possess the right to combine to prevent a rise of wages, while workmen run the risk of heavy punishment should they unite to obtain an advance in wages?

Why should the old law of the maximum still

weigh upon bread, while it does not weigh upon corn?
Why should the capitalist be unable to lend his money
at more than 5 or 6 per cent., while nothing hinders
him from letting his house for 20 or 30 per cent.?

These are some of the questions which spontaneously presented themselves to the good sense of our
new statesmen. They have taken up several others
of which the enumeration would be too long here,
but which are all under consideration, and which we
shall see settled sooner or later.

It does not belong to me to prognosticate in what
space of time or in what order, the will which rules
us may take these problems in hand. To do good is
not everything; it must be done at the right time,
in making allowance for public and private interests.
Every monopoly is worthy of being destroyed, but
when a monopoly is a source of indispensable revenue
to the State, it cannot be abolished as an abuse till
after it has been replaced as a return. Every privilege is worthy of being suppressed, but in one case
the pure and simple return to ordinary law would
entail the spoliation of numerous individuals; in
another, society would lose guarantees it still believes
to be indispensable.

What we can affirm is, that henceforth all personal, industrial, and commercial liberties are accorded us in principle. Some have already passed

within the domain of facts; inquiry has been instituted respecting the others.

. In a few years we have obtained the abolition of passports, that is to say, the right to come and go without control; the liberty of baking, of acting as butchers, of printing, of publishing, and of conducting dramatic entertainments; the abolition of the monopoly which governed the Paris cabs; the right of combination which permits working men to struggle with arms of courtesy, but on a par with, their masters; the liberty of brokerage; the termination of the maximum which regulated the sale of bread; a radical revolution in the Customs' system.

All these laws and decrees are inspired by the same idea; it is the prudent and progressive application of a single principle.

The burdensome institutions, some of which have just been abolished, others modified, and others openly shaken, were all legacies of the past. In an unsettled state of society everything might be displaced in a day, and more logical foundations chosen, but an entire mass of errors and abuses subsists; for a long time the tyranny of anterior facts must be endured. On the celebrated night of the 4th of August, privileges and corrupt appointments were suppressed together. Grades in the army and magisterial functions were gratuitously distributed

by the ruling power to those who appeared worthy
of them. As for the offices which, properly speaking, are industries, every citizen was free to hold
them. The stock-broker, the broker, the auctioneer,
&c., are but middle-men between the seller and the
buyer. A middle-man is but a sort of producer,
like any other; whoever wished to play the part was
welcome.

The strong discipline of the government of the
First Empire aimed at guaranteeing the interests of
every one in giving to these enfranchised workers
the quality and obligations of public servants. This
was the fashion of the day. But, at least, Napoleon did
not pledge the future. The ruling power may create
the places it deems necessary, but it implicitly reserves to itself the right to reduce or abolish them
when they appear to be useless. It accords with equity
that one should proceed considerately in the path
of suppression, and that one should avoid disturb-
ing laborious and honourable existences. Yet subject to these reservations, the State has always the
authority to render to every citizen the use of a
natural right confiscated to the profit of a few.
Suppose that the ministerial officers were still public
servants, that no new engagement had been entered
into by the State, from Napoleon I. to Napoleon
III. it would now suffice to suppress with a stroke

of the pen, without compensation, a gratis privilege.

But on the 28th of April, 1816, the government of the Restoration, being pressed for money, conceived the notion of borrowing several millions from ministerial officers. It said to them, "If you will furnish caution-money, you will be allowed to nominate your successors, or, in other terms, to sell your offices." There was no hesitation in closing with so advantageous a bargain, and at a stroke the ministerial officers became the proprietors of their appointments. On that day the Government thought fit to borrow at three per cent., and made an excellent bargain. Now the caution-money of stock-brokers (to cite but one instance) then amounted to 125,000 francs; that was fifty years ago; during fifty years each payment of caution-money yielded to the treasury an annual profit of two per cent., or 2500 francs yearly, or 125,000 francs every half-century. And the stock-brokers' appointments, which the State has pledged itself to buy up, are each worth nearly two millions in Paris.

The Custom-houses which abounded on our frontier, prior to the late treaties of commerce, these formidable Custom-houses, armed with absolute prohibitions and tolls quasi-prohibitive, were also legacies of the past.

By what series of arguments did kings, the

shepherds of the people, arrive at conclusions like the following: "At two paces from ourselves a certain excellent product is manufactured, far better than all those which we make of the same sort. This is why I forbid you to use it, for my first duty is to protect your interests."

Or, better still: "That fabric, made in London, is not much better than our own; you may then make use of it without inconvenience, and I authorize you to buy it, but it has the defect of costing twenty-five per cent. less than our products of a similar kind; it is necessary then, in your interest, that it should pay an import duty of thirty-three per cent."

Or even: "Meat is scarce and dear, the people are badly fed. This is why no one must go and procure an ox in a foreign country, in order to bring it into this kingdom, under penalty of a fine of fifty-five francs."

One does not argue irrationally for the pleasure of being absurd, and there is no error which is not justified by some good intention. The Custom-house system which, thanks to Heaven, has had its day, was dignified with the fine name of the protective system.

Political power, or the government, was instituted to provide for the collective and indi-

vidual security of citizens against external enemies
and internal evil-doers; that is its part. But
princes have long, far too long, thought that they
were bound to enter into the minutest details, and
to cast their protection over the petty interests of
our kitchen and shop. Protect national industry!
Protect national agriculture! Protect national commerce! And protect also the national consumption,
for all citizens are not necessarily agriculturists,
manufacturers, or merchants, whilst they are all
obliged to be consumers, from their birth till their
death.

The French do not hate being protected; they
are a people of a monarchial temperament. But
they do not all interpret protection in the same way.

"Protect me!" says the agriculturist. "I have
had a good grain harvest; my neighbours, less fortunate, have barely doubled their seed. Before a
month is over prices will rise, if the information in
my newspaper be accurate. I hope to get thirty
francs the hectolitre, and empty my granary under
the best conditions in the world. I shall do this
unless, through culpable weakness, the door is
opened to foreign grain! America threatens us,
Egypt holds plenty suspended over our heads like
the sword of Damocles; Odessa, infamous Odessa,
thinks to glut us with her produce. Help! Let

the door be shut! Or, if you permit the importation of foreign grain, have the humanity to tax it
heavily, in order that the cost of purchasing on the
spot, the transport, and the import duty should raise
the price to thirty francs the hectolitre! If everything goes on as I should wish, I count upon pro-
ceeding to Switzerland, and bringing back four pairs
of oxen."

"Protect me!" says the grazier. "Shut the door
upon foreign cattle, if you wish me to earn a livelihood. We are promised a rise in the price of meat, and
I count upon it; but the admission of Italian, Swiss,
German, Belgian, and English cattle would create
plenty for everybody and be my ruin. Protect
me by prohibiting or by taxing all the products
which come into competition with me. Let grain
enter; I do not grow any, and I like to buy bread
cheaply. Permit the entry, free of duty, of the combustibles with which I warm myself, the glass out of
which I drink, the furniture which I use, the stuffs
with which I clothe myself, and all manufactured
products in general. Oh, visible providence of citizens,
arrange so that I shall not have any competition to
fear as producer, but that in what I consume I may
enjoy all the benefits of competition."

"Protect me!" says the manufacturer. "Cause all
the products which compete with mine to be seized at

8

the frontier; or, if you suffer them to enter, load them with a duty which will render them unsaleable. The interest of the country enjoins upon you to serve my personal interest. Do you not take pity upon the national industry doubly menaced by superior qualities and lower prices? My foreign comrades may reduce me to destitution by inundating France with good merchandise at cheap rates. As a citizen I fear no one in Europe; as a manufacturer I am afraid of everybody. The feeblest foreigner is stronger than I. Strive then that I may preserve the monopoly of my products; but be generous as regards all that which I buy but do not sell. Allow grain to enter, in order that my workmen, being fed for next to nothing, may be satisfied with low wages. Allow the raw materials I employ to enter, and the machines which assist my labour."

"Do nothing of the kind," exclaims the machine-maker. "If the foreigner should come and compete with me, there will be nothing for it but to shut up shop. Stop, or tax, the products which resemble mine; content yourself with opening the door to the metals I use, and you will usefully protect the national industry as far as I am concerned."

"Hold, there!" replies the iron-master. "If foreign iron be admitted, I must put out my furnaces. Leave me the monopoly of my industry; only allow me to import freely the minerals and combustibles which are my instruments of labour."

"No, a hundred times no!" reply the shareholders in mines and coalpits, and the proprietors of forests. "Is our industry less worthy of protection than the others? Now we shall be ruined if foreigners are permitted to introduce plenty and low prices amongst us."

Deafened by such a concert, it is not surprising that statesmen should have been induced to tax all imported articles, or nearly all. Under a tutelary government which concentrated so to speak the people's initiative and responsibility in the chief's hands, the chief thought that he did well in according to each industry the kind of protection it desired. The mass of consumers, eaten up by all these privileges, did not know enough to put its fingers on the mischief, and besides, it had no voice in the council.

Old social economy supported the protective system by patriotic arguments. It thought that the prosperity of a people was measured by the quantity of money it possessed, that it became impoverished by purchasing, that it became enriched by selling, that the acquirer was the tributary of the merchant, and that the best governed countries were those which supplied everything from their own resources without asking anything from others. Such was the doctrine of the most enlightened Frenchmen in the seventeenth century and even up to the middle of the eighteenth.

Boileau congratulated Louis XIV. upon having mulcted " our neighbours of these servile tributes which the luxury of our cities pays to their arts." *

Voltaire in the " Man of Forty Crowns " explained the poverty of France by the amount of our importations. "Four millions must be paid to our neighbours for one article, and five or six for another, in order to put into our noses a filthy powder coming from America. Coffee, tea, chocolate, cochineal, indigo, spices, cost us more than sixty millions annually. We see a hundred times more diamonds in the ears, on the neck, on the hands of the ladies of Paris and of our great cities than were possessed by all the ladies at the court of Henry IV., including the queen. Nearly all these superfluities have had to be paid for in hard cash."

When simple utterances of this character were signed by the greatest genius in the nation, can we wonder that the king thought he was acting well in tightening the chain of Custom-houses around us ?

* Nos voisins de ces tributs serviles
Que payait à leurs arts le luxe de nos villes.

Note that the protective system, which was deemed wise, was a source of revenue to the government. By performing a good action, the king did an excellent stroke of business. The pleasure was two-fold. The more he strictly protected national industry, the more he swelled the budget. And the Customs' duties were among those indirect contributions which the economists of the day preferred to all others, because the consumer paid them, so to speak, unwittingly.

Consider, moreover, that at that time the interdependence of the human race only existed as a dream in the brains of certain fools. A national selfishness prevailed, as was shown in politics by the dread of being conquered (the European equilibrium) and in economy by the dread of being ruined, to the profit of foreign nations. Wisdom consisted in causing the money of others to enter our country, and in shutting the door against the foreign merchandise which might come and draw away our money. To oblige French citizens to pay ten crowns for that which was worth five across the frontier, was playing the foreigner a trick. In this way the ruling power was certain that everybody would confine himself to national products, and that, should an Anglomaniac get his clothes from London or his razors from Birmingham, he would indemnify the nation by paying the duty.

But the foreigner used reprisals and taxed our products as heavily as we had taxed his. The war of tariffs went on during profound peace, and the people bore the brunt, according to custom. The more our kings forced us to pay dearly for the products of English manufacturers, the more did the kings of England make their people pay dearly for our wine and other products. Custom's patriotism rose by degrees to the exaggeration which Benjamin Constant called the enthusiasm for rising prices.

Posterity will be greatly surprised to learn from some old tariff, or still better from the luminous discussions of Michel Chevalier, that at the outset of the Second Empire a ton of steel, designed for the manufacture of the most indispensable tools, paid 1320 francs minimum duty at the French frontier; that bed coverlets were taxed at 220 francs the 100 kilos; that carpets paid as much as 550 francs; that foreign marble, the sole kind a sculptor can use, was weighted with a duty of 742 francs 50 centimes for a statue two metres high.

But it will learn at the same time that our statesmen courageously judged, condemned, and abolished, despite the interested opposition of thousands, a protective system which chiefly protected the decay of industry and the poverty of the people. Decay, because native producers, masters of the home market, secured by exorbitant tariffs or formal prohibition against foreign competition, conducted themselves in their manufactories like feudal lords in their domains. Nothing compelled them to perfect their products, since these products had not to suffer by comparison. They were under no necessity to sell cheaply, since similar products, even were the foreigner to give them away, could not affect the consumer's choice.

By protecting the manufacturer's large profits, a draught was made on the consumer's purse, and the consumer, as we have stated, was everybody. If you take the useful things, which are articles of commerce, one by one, you will see that those who produce them are infinitely less numerous than those who consume them. If it be the interest of ten persons to sell dearly, one hundred thousand persons have an equal interest in paying cheaply for them. Therefore the true protective system is that which permits the consumer to lay in a stock at the lowest possible rates, whether at home or abroad.

Liberty can alone teach nations the industry for which they are fitted, and determine national vocations.

The individual would be a fool if he professed to build his house, grow his provisions, make his own clothes and shoes, in order to free himself from those "servile tributes," which he pays morning and evening to the labour of others; nations would act absurdly in wishing to produce all that they require. It is enough that they put themselves in a position to purchase what they want. Soil, climate, race, education determine the industrial or productive faculties of every country. Let us not strain our talents, let us exercise them as far as they will go, and let us not blush at taking from our neighbours, on condition of a return being made, that which we cannot furnish for ourselves. A certain people is admirably situated for producing meat, iron, pottery, and Dickens's novels, but Nature denies it wine, oil, silk, industrial art, and the comedies of Dumas the Younger. Let it produce in superabundance the things which cost least to its soil and its temperament, and let it send us its surplus in exchange for ours.

Universal Exhibitions would be huge painful spectacles if their result sooner or later were not absolute freedom of commerce. We should inflict the torture of Tantalus on the consumer were we to tell him, "This is what is made at your country's door; it only costs so much; but you wish to buy it, you must pay a fine of 15 per cent." The Custom-house officers, who watch at the gates of these bazaars of the civilized world, have always produced upon us the effect of a living contradiction: *Attolite portas, principes, vestras!* Princes, open the gates, and progress will make the round of the world.

CHAPTER VII.

MONEY.

HERE is an anecdote which struck my attention when I was very little, and which made me reflect before the time.

It was in the first days of January, 1840. A poor man, one of those who conceal their poverty under a black coat, was resisting the demands of a creditor with difficulty. The creditor, his neighbour, had lent him twenty francs for a month; six months had elapsed, and he was unable to repay the twenty francs. If the borrower were poor, the lender was not rich; urged by some pressing need, he made a scene, as it is called. A little girl of twelve being attracted by the noise, guessed the cause of the dispute, entered the adjoining room and reappeared with a large illustrated book, with gilt edges. She said to the creditor, "Sir, here is a book my godfather gave me as a New Year's gift, it is worth

twenty francs; take it; now we are quits." Her
father was moved even to tears; the neighbour felt
himself mollified; he shrugged his shoulders, took
up his hat and went off. When we were alone, the
girl turned towards her father, and said to him,
" Why did not he take it? He would now have been
paid." " No, my little darling." " And why not?"
" It was money which I borrowed from him, and it
is money which I must return to him." " But my
book is well worth twenty francs; it is written on
the cover, and my godfather gave twenty francs for
it. What matters it to that man whether he receives
twenty francs or a thing worth them?" " It is of
great consequence, my child, and the proof is that he
would have accepted twenty francs if you had them
to offer, while he has refused your book." " Then,
papa, money is worth more than other things which
are worth as much as it? How can that be?" Her
father reflected for a moment, and replied, " Everybody is not in want of illustrated books, and everybody is in want of money. If you were to go and
offer your book to the butcher, the baker, the wine-
merchant, the fruiterer, these worthy people would
all tell you that they had opened their shops in the
street to attract pieces of money. The bookseller
himself, who supplied your godfather with the
volume, would not take it back from you at the same

price ; he would tell you, My business is not to purchase, but to sell. Suppose, on the contrary, that
you had twenty francs in real money in your pocket,
you might make your choice among all the things
sold at twenty francs. You might ask at pleasure
for fifty kilos of bread, or twenty-five litres of wine,
or ten metres of stuff like your gown, or three pairs
of shoes, or a book like the one given you as a New
Year's gift. Everybody would hasten to serve you,
because everybody, as I have told you, is in want of
money. Do you understand ? " " I understand that
money has the right of making its choice." " You
have hit upon it." " Oh, Horrid money ! " " Because
we have not any. But if one day I gain as much by
my labour as I hope, you will be astonished at the
services it can render, and you will say, Charming
money ! "

Eight or nine years after this trifling adventure,
I had left college ; I had read, translated, and got by
heart a certain number of classical tirades against
rascally money ; I was filled with admiration, like
so many others, for the laws of Lycurgus and his
iron money ; it had not been forgotten to teach
me that poverty is the fountain of all the virtues.
However, instead of blessing fortune for compelling
me to drink from this consecrated fountain, I often
rebelled against the unequal division of riches : I

asked by what strange privilege the silver, of which
I had not a grain, should procure all the good things
of the world for its possessors? I had heard it said
(as you no doubt have) that silver is nothing by itself;
that it acquires all its value from an understanding;
that nations have selected it as the representative
token of wealth ; that kings have arbitrarily assigned
to it a particular value. Certain newspapers of 1848
had penetrated through the walls of our Lyceum ;
certain diatribes led us to understand that all the
holders of silver made tools of, or tyrannized over,
the people who had none of it ; we saw at the horizon
the light of certain utopias which were to emancipate man from the vile metal, and my heart swelled
with joy at the prospect of universal prosperity
through the medium of paper money. In fine, I was
as unversed in social economy as all the bachelors
of letters of my time and as nearly all the Frenchmen of our time.

One morning the petty chances of travel caused
me to stop in a canton of Finistère where silver is
extracted from the earth. Picture to yourself a
gloomy landscape, a desolate land, an accursed spot,
where it rains five days out of six. The mine
yielded silver lead ore, that is to say lead mixed with
silver. To work it, machines and buildings had been
constructed at great cost; two engineers, two fore-

men, a multitude of dirty and wretched workers, lived in this moist hell, remote from everything. I descended with them to the bottom of their subterranean workshops; I followed them, lamp in hand, along the dismal levels where the earth, badly propped up, flowed down in mud upon our heads. When we had re-ascended to the light of day, an amiable and hospitable engineer conducted us to the furnaces where the lead was extracted from the ore, thence to the laboratory where the silver was separated from the lead. A few ingots of silver, taken from the crucible, were ready to enter into circulation.

Do you remember the tirade of Robinson Crusoe, when, on searching the inexhaustible ship, he laid hands upon the captain's stock of coin? "Here you are, then, vile metal,—vile metal." Well, then, I must admit, my impression was quite different. These unfortunate ingots, which had cost my fellow-men so much trouble, struck me with a certain respect. Silver appeared to me, for the first time, as a product laboriously torn from the earth. I passed in review all the professions which yield it to man, and I did not observe one more hard than that of these miners. I said to myself, "The fact is, that silver is more easily earned than produced : these ingots cost very dear."

As I had thought aloud the engineer replied to

me, "They cost so much that, most likely, we shall make none in the coming year. Even the lead, which furnishes the greater portion of our returns, barely covers the expense of working. They speak about abandoning the mine; this is unfortunate for all these worthy folks who earn their bread from it." "Abandon a mine which yields silver! Is that possible?" "Indeed, if you had a field which it did not pay to cultivate, would you persist in tilling it? Silver, like corn, is the product of labour. The difference is that the one is reaped from the surface of the earth, and the other from its depths. The one furnishes you with bread for your soup, the other a pleasant and wholesome spoon to take it with."

He mentioned to me some silver mines which had been abandoned for the same reason that fields utterly worn out are not cultivated. I learned with astonishment that not only in Europe, but in America, the production of silver is always costly, frequently ruinous, and that in no part of the world is the vile metal to be picked up by the first comer. I said to him, "Thus the frightful mass of silver which encumbers the earth under every shape, coin, silver plate, silver lace, silvered articles, and the rest, has been the product of labour as repugnant, as tedious, as thankless as this here?" "You need not doubt it. Metallurgical processes vary a little: here we have recourse to smelting, in other places amalgamation is employed; the engineers of Freyberg are rather more skilful than those of Guanaxato, but the miner's labour is everywhere equally hard, and you will not find a piece of ten sous which has not cost at least ten drops of sweat. Besides, the precious metals are not as abundant as you think on the surface of the globe. One of our most illustrious masters, M. Michel Chevalier, has calculated that all the silver extracted from the mines of the New World would make a sphere of forty metres in circumference, in other words, a ball which, placed at the foot of the Vendôme Column, would conceal exactly two-thirds of its height." "So little? Yet a Titan could carry that on his shoulders." "Mythology," he smilingly replied, "has omitted to tell us how many horse-power each Titan represented. But rest assured of this, that several millions of labourers have died of the task of rolling this snow-ball on to us." "Poor people! Frightful labour! And for whom? For a handful of parasites and idlers." The engineer looked at me, smiled again, and said, "No man is such a fool as to throw the products of his labour to idlers and parasites. You see these ingots; I have done my part, like all those who have helped, directly or not, in extracting them from the earth. Detach, in your mind, a morsel of about two kilogrammes: that is my last month's salary. What shall I do with it? I shall give a portion to those who feed me, another to those who clothe me, another to the good woman who washes my linen, another to the servant who takes care of my house. In short, I shall exchange this silver, the price of my labour, for the labour of twenty persons. The workmen who act here under my orders will do exactly as I do. Each will receive a fractional part of these ingots, and will divide it around him in exchange for other things. We are manufacturers, we create a product, we divide it among ourselves pro rata according to our respective co-operation; then we employ our portion in remunerating the services which we cannot render to ourselves. In the neighbouring market-town there is a baker who heats his oven at the hour we light our lamps. He is no idler, still less a parasite, and you would be very wrong in quarrelling with him, even were all these ingots now before you to be carried into his shop. He works for us, and we work for him. Now, you may hold it for certain that all the silver in the world is distributed according to the same law, from the moment that ingots leave the mine. As soon as extracted, so soon are they divided among those who have given form to them. As soon as divided, so soon are they exchanged for things and services of all kinds."

This conversation raised silver in my esteem; it

taught me to consider the vile metal as one of the most interesting products of human energy.

Some years later I met (also in France) a worthy man who occupied himself in producing gold. He was an Alsatian, one of those gold seekers of the Rhine, who look for the metal in the gravel of the river. His business consisted in washing, beneath the current, some kilogrammes of sand selected from likely spots, in order to sift out the specks of gold. It was hard work, and in addition, rather thankless : rheumatism was chiefly reaped from it. Not that the specks were rare : in each cubic metre of average gravel you will find about 40,000, but they are so light that the stream carries many from Switzerland to Strasburg, across the Lake of Constance, without letting them drop by the way. From 17,000 to 22,000 of these specks are required to make a gramme of gold, about the value of three francs. My gold seeker earned on an average 1 franc 75 centimes a day. He has left off work to go to field labour, at which he will get 10 sous more. Thus gold is a product which may cost more than its worth.

It is the most widely diffused of all metals, after iron which colours our fields and our rocks, the blood of man, and the leaf of the beech, but it is so greatly scattered, and is reduced into such small fractions, that often the amount extracted does not pay for the labour.

However, you will say, there are countries where one has but to stoop to pick it up. Australia! California! Are the riches of the New World but an empty word?

No. The New World has supplied a considerable mass of gold, seeing that all the metal extracted from its mines from the time of Columbus up to last year, would fill a chamber of seven square metres by five in height.* But this result, which may not, perhaps, appear to you very imposing, is the price of incalculable labour. You have heard it said that in that country the grains of gold carried along by the brooks and torrents weighed infinitely more than the specks of the Rhine. That is true. You have been told that on a particular day, at a particular place, a pioneer has accidentally found a nugget which was a fortune. Agreed. There is a little more adventure, a little less industry, properly so called, in the search after gold than in the working of a silver mine. Nevertheless, I maintain that gold is a product in the most honourable sense of the word.

In all man's enterprises there is uncertainty: planting cabbages is leaving something to chance.

* Michel Chevalier, *la Monnaie,* 2nd edition, p. 561.

The adventurer who rushes in pursuit of gold among the Rocky Mountains is a producer by the same title as the market-gardener of Vincennes; he moves towards the same end, which is to increase the sum of useful things, but he proceeds by shorter and more dangerous paths. If he lays his hand upon a nugget worth 200,000 francs (that has happened), bear in mind that he has not met with this luck without undergoing privations, fatigue, and perils. He has made long journeys, suffered from hunger and thirst, risked his life twenty times. This is to labour otherwise than, but quite as much as, the peaceable gardener who handles his spade and watering-pot. Nature gives nothing gratis, not even nuggets of 200,000 francs. Besides, the working of rich deposits becomes less precarious from day to day, and more business-like in its form. A placer now-a-days does not imperfectly resemble our great manufactories. The quartz is there crushed by steam machinery; the raw material is washed in channels of water fashioned at a great cost; chemical manipulations are there conducted in spacious laboratories; the expenses of the establishment are enormous, the products consumed in the manufacture cost extremely dear; the annual profit of the manufactory is the surplus of the receipts over the expenses, as in an iron foundry or a spinning-mill.

If you remember, we gave a lengthy explanation of the sense of the verb, to produce. It means to carry on to the end, that is to say, to snatch things from Nature's niggard breast, and put them into the consumer's hands.

You know that things have the more value the greater the demand for them and the smaller the supply.

Gold and silver have been in demand since ever they were known. Why? Because they are incomparably more beautiful than all the other metals; because they are unchanged by air, by water, and nearly all acids; because they may be almost indefinitely preserved upon the earth and under it, and are found unaltered in the sixty-century-old mummy chest. Gold and silver are in demand because they furnish material for the most brilliant ornaments, for the healthiest and most serviceable utensils. Their inconceivable malleability is not foreign to the favour they enjoy. You know that gold can be reduced to leaves so fine that nine hundred must be placed the one upon the other to make the thickness of a millimètre. This property of the most glittering of metals permits us to give a little cheerfulness to the insides of the humblest houses. A single gramme of silver, worth about twenty centimes, may be stretched out into wire, without breaking, two and a half kilometres in length. With two grammes of gold, worth less than seven francs, we may coat a silver wire five hundred leagues long. Is it surprising, then, that materials endowed with such marvellous attributes should have been in request from the infancy of the human race? Scarcely do we possess necessaries than we go in quest of superfluities. And the precious metals were without question the most desirable superfluities before the arts were discovered. Hence gold and silver were eagerly sought for wherever they were displayed. Do I require to add that they were much less offered?

The richest mines in the world were unknown in Europe; chemistry did not exist, metallurgy was in its infancy. A few pieces of native silver, a few grains of gold gathered from the bed of a stream, —these were the first elements which came to be used in exchange. On what footing? At what price? I can hardly venture to guess. Remember that the value of the precious metals has constantly fallen since the earliest historic period, for they became more plentiful and were more largely supplied from day to day; remember that America has been discovered for three centuries and a half; that we have been in full communication with Australia and California for more than twelve years; that European civilization possesses a stock of silver and gold valued at forty milliards, and that, despite all this, he who should give up a kilogramme of gold in France at the present day would get in exchange six or seven thousand kilogrammes of corn! For a single kilogramme of gold more bread may be purchased than eight thousand men can eat in a day!

Carry yourself back forty centuries, and try to figure to yourself the mass of things which could then be obtained in exchange for a kilogramme of gold!

The attention of men had been necessarily turned to these admirable products; they were closely studied. The means of refining them pretty well were discovered; it was shown that they were simple bodies, everywhere and always identical when in the pure state. One learned to recognize them, not only by their colour, their ring, and their weight, but by more infallible signs. One ascertained by reflection that these products were those which contained the greatest value in the smallest compass; they were more easily transported, preserved, and hidden, than all other things. Saving adopted them, fear stored them up. The man of all ages desires to guard what he possesses. In every age also, the sensible worker thinks about laying up a store for the future. But how is he to secure himself against the privations of declining years?

Provisions of all kinds spoil by keeping,—food, clothes, and the rest. Besides, all these things would be of prodigious bulk, and the largest savings would attract the first robbers.

The wisest among men then framed an argument which cannot be too much admired : "Since there are metals which everybody desires, and which are always in request in the general market; since these things are incorruptible and therefore easily preserved ; comprise large value in a small compass, and are consequently as easily concealed as carried; let us exchange our savings for ingots of gold or silver. In this manner we shall transform the surplus of our harvests, the added value of our services, into solid, imperishable, and perpetually exchangeable things, seeing that the human race never has enough of them."

The Dutchman is greatly admired, and not without reason, who thought fit to salt his herring. Before his day every draught of fish somewhat miraculous, was a good thing three-parts wasted. Fish does not keep long in store ; it must be eaten at once, or it will turn bad. Thanks to salting, it can be kept for three months, six months, an entire year.

But shall we refuse a word of praise to the first fisherman who said to himself, "My catch is too large ; it is impossible for me to consume the whole of it. It is true that I can barter the surplus with the good people of the neighbourhood who like fish. One will give me vegetables, another bacon, another cloth, another bread ; but how full my larder would be then ! How can I ever get through the whole myself? Shall I have to exchange over again ? Shall I let them spoil ? I may as well let my fish rot at once. An idea strikes me. What if I exchanged all that for a small ingot of silver or gold, which would be worth my ten thousand herrings ! The metal will not spoil, I can keep it, and exchange it bit by bit, sometimes for a sole, sometimes for a lobster, when I am too old to go a-fishing myself." The first who argued thus was no fool, you must admit ; he had found the way to salt his herring without salt.

When the experience of several centuries had shown that the merits of gold and silver were alloyed with no drawback, what probably happened was that the two things most in demand served to measure the value of all the others.

Must we say, the two ? It is supposed that, in Europe, silver was first used to concentrate savings and measure values. Gold was too scarce and too dear to enter into general circulation. Let us confine ourselves to silver, then, and see the new use made of it.

9

After having been an article of luxury, it had become an instrument to preserve,.a means of carefully guarding in a small compass the equivalent of all the things which one wished to save.   But a step had to be taken to make it the principal equivalent, as some certain dimensions of the human body were the principal measures of length, as a day's labour is still in many places the measure of arable areas.

Every measure is a comparison ; I do not profess to teach you that.   Every comparison implies a type, a common standard by which sizes, surfaces, volumes, weights, and different values are estimated.

To indicate the height of a mountain, the ancients said, it is so many elbow-lengths, that is to say, it is two, three thousand times higher than the fore-arm of an average man, from the tip of the fingers up to the elbow.   To estimate the length of a road, they said, so many steps must be taken before reaching the end.   All nations have begun by employing approximate measures, such as the finger, the palm, the foot, the fathom, the vessel, the pitcher, &c. These standards, rude though they were, rendered man a great service.   Experience soon taught that the best means of comparing two quantities with each other was to compare them with the unit one after the other.

But if it only required a little geometry to measure

lengths, surfaces, and bulks; though the scales suf-
ficed to measure the weights of the most diverse
bodies, the measure of values was far more delicate,
and required the aid of a new instrument. The
diversity of our wants is infinite; infinite is the
diversity of things and services which we produce,
which we consume, which we exchange with each
other. Tell me the means, if you please, of exactly
comparing such different things. How many litres
of corn are there in an hour of music? How many
English pears go to a medical consultation? Is the
day's work of the head of an office worth twenty
kilogrammes of flat sheet iron, or twenty-five?
Would Benvenuto Celini's "Perseus" be paid too
much or too little, if it were exchanged for a house on
the Boulevard Montmartre?

Exchange by barter is progress, the first step in
elementary life. The pure savage is the person who
makes everything for himself—his hut, his garments,
his feet-covering, his bread, his meat with bow and
arrows, his house by blows of the hatchet, his hatchet
by blows of a hammer, his hammer Heaven knows
how, for there is something paradoxical in this
hypothesis, and one cannot conceive a man sufficing
for all his wants without having recourse to exchange.

To devote oneself to the creation of a single

thing, perfect oneself as much as possible in a unique industry, manufacture in abundance the special product which is or which becomes our natural fruit, and barter this surplusage of production for other necessaries of life, is to be but half a savage.

But barter has its drawbacks which are seen at a glance. It greatly complicates the most rudimentary transactions. Endeavour for a moment to picture to yourself not an artificer of luxury, an artist, an advocate, a printer, but a tiller of the soil exercising the most primitive industry. He has six times more corn than he can consume in a year; but he requires meat, salt, wine, spices, clothes, linen, shoes, building materials. For every exchange he has to make, he must seek a man specially prepared. Does he require tiles? slaters abound; but he will have to ask ten, perhaps, before meeting with one who, at the same moment, requires corn. Does he wish to eat beef at his dinner? He must seek and find among the graziers of the neighbourhood one who is in want of corn. But he does not require a whole ox, only a simple piece of three kilos: what has to be done is to bring together a number of other persons and purchase the animal at their common cost. The grazier himself has infinitely varied wants, for he is a man; he asks only to barter his merchandise for all the products required by him; but he is wise, he will not slaughter his beast except for a purpose, when he shall see around him producers of all kinds who make the common offer, under a thousand different forms, of the exact equivalent of his ox. Before that person had ended in assembling this congress of consumers and producers, the unhappy animal (I mean the ox) would have died of old age.

I have taken as examples only products easily divisible and in general consumption. How would it be if the point were to barter a house on the Boulevard, a box at the Opera, a share in a railway? The exchange would occupy more time than the manufacture itself; the worker would exhaust his life in seeking an equivalent for his products, and the world would present the spectacle of a universal blindman's buff.

Humanity took a great step on the day when it invented the unity of value by bringing all things into a common measure of relation. Silver became, so to speak, the intermediary in all exchanges, and the addition of this new element, which seemed at first sight to complicate, simplified them. In the same way that the metre permits us exactly to compare the heights of two distant mountains, for instance, Mont Blanc and Cotopaxi, does the value of a gramme of silver permit us to compare things so different as a doctor's visit and a kilogramme of

arsenic acid.   What is the function of the metre in
the comparison of these sublime heights?   It is
merely a simple intermediary, but an indispensable
intermediary, because all man's efforts would not
lead to bringing these two mountains together, in
the way one places two children back to back to
compare their height.   It is thus that silver, compared successively with all values, furnishes us with
their exact measure and enables us to compare them
with each other.

Is there an appreciable connection between the
washing of two shirts, the journey of a messenger,
ten quires of letter-paper, and a hundred grains of
smoking-tobacco?   None whatever.   But if the laws
of supply and demand ensure the current exchange
of each of these things and services for five grammes
of silver, it clearly follows that on a particular day,
at a particular place, these very diverse services and
things, so slightly capable of comparison the one
with the other, represent identical values.

If everything on sale be valued by the weight of
silver, it follows that all kinds of producers no
longer require to seek direct exchange.   He who
possesses too much corn and not enough wool is not
obliged to run about calling for a dealer in wool, and
crying, "Where is he who has too much wool and
not enough corn?"   He simply puts his corn on

sale, and he finds a thousand purchasers if he find one. The business finished, he puts the silver into his pocket, seeks a seller of wool, and finds a thousand if he find one. He has performed two operations in place of one, two exchanges in place of one, I admit; tell me, however, has not this two-fold operation saved him time and trouble ?

But, perhaps, he has run some risk ? Let us consider the facts. Suppose that, having sold his corn, he should not find any wool to purchase. The operation would then be cut short midway. In that case, would not the corn-factor be a dupe ?

Yes, indeed, he would be one, if silver were but a sign, a representative, an instrument of exchange, as has been said in many places, and as you have possibly fancied yourself. But it is a precious metal, and has been recognized as such from time immemorial, all over the world. If its value were but conventional, it would be nil. No one would be fool enough to accept it in exchange for actual things. Everybody would dread being taken unawares and having given something for nothing, if perchance the convention came to an end. The human race is protected against such an accident ; it knows that no revolution can depreciate a product which measures the value of all others. The man who does not find what he wants for sale, easily resigns himself to keep his silver ;

he does not accuse the society which has left him with it as payment. He stores up a product which is unalterable, incorruptible, which is not affected by damp as corn is, which is in no danger from moths like linen, and which may always be exchanged for things to be disposed of, seeing that it is always and everywhere in demand.

Silver is not precious because it serves to measure values; it is employed to measure values because it is intrinsically precious.

In applying silver to measure values, it is true that its worth has been increased. Demand leads to a rise in price. All the products for which a new use is found become dearer. The price of coal has trebled since it was used in steam-engines ;- the price of silver must have been trebled on the day it was employed as money.

I do not say as material for money. Silver is money by itself, before being coined ; it preserves its monetary quality through all the changes of form, of weight, of name which it may undergo. In itself, exterior to any convention, independently of all laws, prior to the work of the machine which gives it an impress, and after the cost of effacing it, silver possesses a known, recognized, incontestable value, one emi-nently fitted for measuring other values. In this sense it is money. Twenty-two grammes and a half

of virgin silver, or twenty-five grammes of silver
of nine-tenths purity, represent an identical value,
whatever the form and imprint given to them. Make
of them a sphere, a cube, a cone, a disc, a medal, you
will never make them more or less than twenty-two
grammes and a half of virgin silver, exchangeable in
all countries for things or services which are worth
five francs.

Many honest persons imagine, too, that the State,
in impressing the effigy of the Sovereign on a disk
of metal, thereby imparts to it an arbitrary value.
Others, more enlightened, think, however, that coinage sensibly increases the value of the metal; that
the Government deducts a seignorage from the
money it coins. I have been told, and have believed from childhood, that a five-franc piece, when
melted or broken, was not worth more than four
francs fifty centimes.

The truth is that a five-franc piece contains
fine silver to the amount of five francs, minus three
centimes and three-fourths; that the State does not
levy any tax on money coined in France; that,
besides, it is not the State which coins the money,
but a contractor, executing the orders of the citizens
under the absolutely gratuitous supervision of the
State.

All of us have the right to coin money. If you

keep in your cellar an ingot of virgin silver, if you
find in a heritage a lot of old silver plate, you may
carry these things to the contractor, who works
them up; he will convert them into pieces of five-
francs, and that will cost you only one franc fifty
centimes the kilogramme, that is to say, less than
four centimes per piece, as I have already stated.
A kilogramme of silver nine-tenths fine is thus
worth, when coined, two hundred francs, less thirty
sous.

If it were your pleasure to-morrow to re-melt
these forty pieces of five francs in order to make an
ingot, a tureen of them, you would be entitled to do
so, but you would lose the amount it costs to make
them, that is to say, one franc fifty centimes.

In order that a kilogramme of silver, coined at
the mint, should be worth one franc fifty centimes
in excess of an ingot of the same weight and character, the operation of coining must have added to it a
supplement of utility.

In fact, this operation saves us more time and
trouble than the value of one franc fifty centimes.
Place yourself for an instant in the place of a
Parisian bourgeois, who should be obliged to go and
make his purchases with two hundred francs in
ingots.

Before leaving home, he will have to cut up his

silver in pieces of all sizes, which in itself is no trifling job. But once he gets among the tradesmen, what a series of tribulations! Each purchase necessarily implies two operations, the weighing and assaying of the ingot, or the verification of its fineness. Between silver of nine-tenths fineness, and silver of eight, even of seven, there is no difference appreciable by the eyes.

It is true that the buyer might weigh and assay his ingots beforehand, and say, " I warrant you there are so many grammes of a certain fineness." But the tradesman would ask for proof, and he would be right. The grocer would say, " I have weighed my sugar, weigh your silver. I have allowed you to taste my plums, and you wish me to accept your ingots without testing them?"

It may be guessed that, at this rate, transactions would not be speedily concluded. Exchange was notably accelerated on the day that it was agreed to conduct it with ingots weighed beforehand, assayed beforehand, and, moreover, certified by a public authority.

When you enter a shop, and throw a piece of five francs on the counter, the tradesman has only to open his eyes and lend an ear,—all other verification would be superfluous. He instantly knows that the piece weighs twenty-five grammes, that its fineness is nine hundred millièmes, and that, in consequence, he receives twenty-two grains and a half of pure silver. The longest and most minute labour would not yield him any more information. From the time the disk is clothed with the legal stamp, one is sure that it has been manufactured by a responsible contractor, under the eyes of disinterested supervisors.

The piece of five francs is therefore a more serviceable, more available, and more trustworthy article than a disk of the same weight and the same alloy. Are these advantages bought too dearly for three centimes and three-fourths? No, especially if you consider that the outlay of three centimes is spread over more than a thousand transactions.

The cost of fabrication is levied by the contractor in exchange for real work and service. He keeps the rolling-machines, the punches, the stamping-presses going; his factory is a genuine mill, which converts ingots into certificated disks.

The State gratuitously supervises all these coining operates. This supervision being in the interest of the public, it is just and natural that the public should pay all the cost.

You observe that the difference is almost nil between the price of silver in ingots and the price of coined silver. All civilized nations have adopted the same mode of acting; coined silver passes everywhere at its intrinsic value. In international exchanges a deduction is made for the alloy and the impress; the weight of fine silver in each piece is alone taken into account. If you have corn to sell, and if you estimate the hectolitre at ninety grammes of pure silver, it matters little to you whether you are paid in five-franc pieces bearing the effigy of the Emperor of the French, in Prussian thalers, in Austrian florins, or in Indian rupees; the important thing is that you obtain seventy grains of pure silver, certified by no matter what authority. All the monarchies, all the republics comprised in the group of European civilization, are equally deserving of trust in matters relating to coin.

There is thus a common measure, applicable to all values; this is the gramme of fine silver. The unit of value has been found; what the human race still wants is a uniform coinage. The more nations are brought together by exchange, the more is the want of a uniform type felt. When travel was difficult, and commerce was hampered with a thousand obstacles, when each nation saw its most direct enemy in its nearest neighbour, when small and great despots preyed upon their subjects in every way, without disdaining the issue of bad money, it was natural that each one regarded foreign money with misgiving. The coins of one country did not pass current in another; it was necessary to have recourse to a money-changer, that is to say, to give thirty grammes of silver with one effigy for twenty-eight with another.

Shortly afterwards one crossed another frontier, another money had to be employed, and the twenty-eight grammes of metal, in the money-changer's hands, were reduced to twenty-five. If the trip lasted a month, in a country arbitrarily divided like Germany and Italy, the largest piece of money vanished in smoke : the money-changers had taken everything. At the present day one may traverse five hundred leagues in forty-eight hours; the great European family, which includes the United States of America, exchanges more things in a month than our ancestors did in a century; nations draw together with as much zeal as they formerly displayed in remaining asunder ; public finance is everywhere transacted above-board ; thus the time has come for striking a set of coins which would circulate without loss and without hindrance from one end to the other of the civilized world.

Four or five silver medals, of an identical value and a uniform model, would suffice to solve the problem. The face might be indefinitely varied, according to the forms of government and the profiles of different princes; the reverse would indicate by a readable figure the weight of each piece. The numbers 2, 5, 10, 25 would convey to Frenchmen as well as to Russians, to Spaniards as well as to Americans, that they had before their eyes 2, 5, 10, 25 grammes of silver of 900 millièmes purity. Virgin silver is unfitted for the production of good coin; experience has shown that a tenth part of copper and nine-tenths of fine silver constitute the most satisfactory alloy. Civilized nations are accustomed to employ this silver with a decimal of copper; they understand how to reduce it to its exact value by the simplest and most familiar of calculations.

But, whilst economists congratulate themselves on having at last hit upon a universal coinage, a part of the civilized world has selected gold as the common measure of value, and has demonetized silver. How? Why? I shall endeavour to tell you.

You are aware that gold has all the qualities requisite for making good coin. It is a product which is very beautiful, very useful, and is in general demand. Christopher Columbus's savages did not tread it under their feet, as has been alleged; they decorated their persons and their temples with it; they exchanged it for other things.

It is not only more beautiful, but it is also scarcer than silver. Being in larger demand, it is more valuable and contains greater worth in an equal compass.

At this moment a kilogramme of pure gold is exchangeable for fifteen kilogrammes and a half of pure silver. The relation between the two metals is therefore as 1 to 15½.

For the uses of life, in such an advanced state of civilization as ours, gold has one great advantage over silver—it is more portable. A hundred and fifty-five pieces of 20 francs, worth as a whole 3100 francs, weigh one kilogramme only. This is a weight which can be carried in one's pockets without being inconvenient. The same sum, in silver, would weigh fifteen kilogrammes and a half: this is the average burden of a Parisian porter; it is the half of the luggage which each traveller is allowed gratis on our railways. Gold is therefore a money which becomes indispensable in proportion as our wants become complex and refined, as communication increases, as society is enriched.

We produce, we consume, we exchange, we travel far more than the French of the tenth century, for instance ; gold is therefore more essential to us.

Without going so far back, each of us can recur to the happy age when twenty sous in silver ensured him enjoyment for a whole Sunday. How many balls, how much sugar candy and gingerbread could be got for twenty sous! Now we are gentlemen; our wants are more complex; we do not venture to go along the streets of Paris without carrying several twenty-franc pieces with us. The provision of a bourgeois' day would tear our pockets if we carried it in silver.

When a Parisian stops in a village, I mean a real village, he marvels to see how tenacious five-franc pieces are of existence. When a villager ventures to go to Paris, Marseilles, Havre, Bordeaux, he is astonished to see how louis run through his fingers. This is because the Parisian is transplanted to the midst of a life less advanced and also less exacting. His wants diminish for lack of opportunities; he is in a centre where everybody produces less and consumes less. The village is a century and half behind the great towns; gold is almost a superfluity there, as all the wants which can be satisfied in a day scarcely demand the outlay of five francs. The peasant who arrives in the midst of Paris is surrounded by people who gain, expend, and enjoy more than he does; who have more wants, more resources, a more consuming activity, and who look up to gold with the less respect because they have toiled less to obtain it. This parallel represents the civilization of other days and the civilization of the future. The village is the past; the city is the future. There was a time when Paris and Marseilles lived humbly like a hamlet of Brittany or of Alsace; the time will come when the inhabitants of the hamlets will have the same wants and the same resources as the Parisian of the present day. Gold coin will be as indispensable to the villagers of the twentieth century as it was useless to the bourgeois of the tenth.

In our day, you may observe that the usage of gold is visibly increasing. But a century ago the noblest of metals was hardly known to the labouring classes. The Court, the finance department, the higher commerce familiarly handled it; the nobleman in the play said to his servant, "Frontin, put gold into my pockets!" But ordinary folks only touched it with superstitious terror, and merely hid it when they received it. This affectation has lasted to our day; men of my own age can recall the time when tradesmen feared to pay a bill in gold coin. Their credit would have suffered by so doing; it would have been said in the neighbourhood, "Such an one has got to the bottom of his bag: he is bringing up bile." This was due to the supposition that gold was not made to circulate, but to lie at the bottom of drawers. English travellers, who paid for everything in gold, excited scandal in the small towns, and even to some extent in the large ones.

Whence has come the change that has occurred in

our manners? Do you think to explain it by the
marvellous importations from Australia and California? No. The production of gold has been extended, I admit, but that of silver has not fallen off
during the same period. In order that a kilogramme
of gold can now be exchanged for fifteen kilogrammes
and a half of silver, it was requisite that the influx
of the two materials should have remained in an
almost fixed proportion. In other words, it is clear
that we have received from Mexico, or elsewhere,
about thirty-one pounds of fine silver every time that
Australia or California sent us a kilogramme of gold:
had this not happened the respective value of the
two metals would have sensibly altered, and no one
would any longer give four five-franc pieces in silver
for a piece of twenty francs in gold. If the proportion has remained the same, or nearly so, since 1848,
it is because we have rather more gold than formerly,
and enormously more silver.

And yet it is gold which circulates; it is silver
which is piled up or buried, or exported, or slumbers
in ingots in cellars. The result may be easily de-
duced. If France partially gives up using the
heaviest of the precious metals, if all the citizens
who take ingots to the Mint carry gold thither,
this is because it better suits the wants of the
times; this is because a more portable metal better

answers the purpose of a people increasing in enterprise.

The gold pieces are coined for private persons, like the silver pieces. The contractors obtain 6 francs 70 centimes the kilogramme, or nearly four centimes on a piece of 20 francs, rather more than one centime on a piece of five francs. Therefore the gold piece of five francs has an intrinsic value of about 4 francs 99 centimes. Coined gold of 900 millièmes fine, that is to say, containing a tenth part of copper, is still more solid and more unalterable than coined silver.

The gramme of gold might serve as the basis of all values, and become the base of a universal coinage, quite as well as the gramme of silver. "How much would you take to make me a coat?" "Thirty-six grammes of gold, as nearly as possible." "How much is this pair of horses worth?" "Two kilogrammes of gold." "A house on the Boulevard Haussmann was sold yesterday morning for 1000 kilogrammes sterling gold, that is to say, gold of 999 millièmes fineness." One would be soon accustomed to this mode of counting.

The difficulty would consist in estimating a packet of tobacco, a metre of calico, a litre of Argenteuil wine, in grammes of gold.

A scale founded on the gramme of silver might

express the largest values; a series starting from the gramme of gold is necessarily more limited; it could not go below 3 francs 10 centimes; moreover, coins of 3 francs 10 centimes in gold would be liable to be blown away. Silver itself cannot be made small enough to pay for a roll of bread or a box of lucifer matches. A piece of five centimes in silver would weigh 25 centigrammes, and would properly belong to the world of small things. Despite this imperfection, which compels the use of copper coin, silver is not only useful, but is indispensable as a measure of values under five francs.

Thus, civilization is armed with two instruments marvellously well adapted for measuring values. Gold, taken by itself, is an admirable money: its sole defect is that it only serves to estimate things of a high price. Silver, in its way, is an irreproachable money, excepting that it occupies too much space and weighs too heavily.

Silver can value everything, starting from fifty centimes; gold can value everything, starting from five francs. Alas! the hard thing is to employ these two privileged things, which estimate all others, for valuing each other.

In countries where silver is adopted as the standard, that is to say, as the sole measure of values, silver values everything, purchases everything—corn, cloth, wine ; gold itself is there classed among merchandise. All these things rise and fall according to supply and demand ; less or more is given in exchange for a gramme of silver. Silver alone never fluctuates; it represents the fixed, invariable unity, by which values of all sorts are estimated. If I conclude a long-dated bargain, if for instance I lend to a lay society or a religious association a hundred kilogrammes of silver conditionally on receiving five per cent. annually in perpetuity, I am certain that my most remote posterity will receive every year five kilogrammes of the same metal. This contract, like all contracts in the world, gives a scope to the chance of circumstances, it involves a share in the unknown. I cannot foresee whether, in two or three centuries, food, clothes, silver plate, the objects of primary necessity, the merchandise of luxury, will be more or less costly than in my own day. Perhaps one will be able to obtain for a gramme of silver four times as much bread as one can buy with it to-day ; perhaps one will obtain four times less ; that is the doubtful part of the business. What is not doubtful is that my heirs will be entitled to a yearly payment of five kilogrammes of silver identical with those I lent.

· In a country where gold is the sole standard of value, it is gold which values and purchases all kinds of merchandise, corn as well as silver. Suppose a contract at long date, twenty kilogrammes of gold being lent for a perpetual annuity at 5 per cent., the heirs of the lender are assured of a clear and invariable return ; they will receive every year a kilogramme. of gold. Nothing can prove that this kilogramme will purchase to the end of all things 8000 kilogrammes of corn ; perhaps in a hundred years 20,000 will be given for it, perhaps only 5000 ; but one is certain that the heirs will perpetually receive an equal weight of an identical metal. This security is not to be despised.

Suppose, on the other hand, a country where the unit of value is what it has been among us since the introduction of the metrical system, and you will see very curious complications arise.

The great legislators of the year XI, being justly convinced that gold alone would constitute but an incomplete coinage, that silver alone would constitute but an inadequate coinage, did not wish to demonetize either the one metal or the other. They did well ; gold and silver are two indispensable elements in commercial transactions. But they made a mistake in establishing two standards, the one of gold and the other of silver, in deciding that the unit of value might be indifferently either a piece of silver weighing five grammes, or the twentieth part of a piece of gold weighing six grammes 45,161 hundred millièmes.

To determine that a particular weight of silver should always be equal to a particular weight of gold was to decree in some respects the identity of the two metals in unequal measure, that is to say, that a kilogramme of gold and fifteen kilogrammes and a half of silver were one and the same; it was to discredit beforehand the events which might vary a casual, temporary, and local proportion; in a word, it was to do violence to nature.

M. Michel Chevalier, in a book which I ought to cite at every line, takes exception with eloquent logic to the system of the double standard. I refer to his argumentation those who wish to get to the bottom of this question, and I confine myself to skimming it here.

Gold and silver have no relationship; they are not the eldest or the younger son of an aristocratic family. The distance which separates them as regards value may vary to infinity. In the same country one sees, according to the period, the kilogramme of gold become exchangeable for ten, twelve, fourteen, fifteen, seventeen, eighteen kilogrammes of silver. During the same period the proportion is not everywhere the same. In 1857, when commerce opened the gates of Japan, the natives exchanged a kilogramme of gold for three kilogrammes of silver and one-seventh. This meant that gold compared with silver was five times cheaper at Yeddo than at Paris. You would have quintupled your capital by carrying your silver to Japan and exchanging it for gold.

Nothing proves that among ourselves the proportion of 1 to 15½ will be maintained even approximatively as it has been for half a century. The respective scarcity of the two metals is an important element in their price. Let another California be discovered, or let.two or three silver mines be stopped, gold will superabound, become depreciated; silver will grow scarce; the demand for it being in excess of the supply, it will rise in price.

At such a juncture every shrewd debtor will proceed to repay his creditors. Only he will pay them in gold what he borrowed from them in silver. All the guardians who know how to reckon will hasten to emancipate their wards, being too happy to repay in depreciated gold the trust funds they received in silver. All who have annuities to pay will discharge them in gold, and thus rid themselves of legal liability at half price. Creditors, wards, annuitants will call out that they are being ruined. They will be answered, "Of what do you complain? So many francs are due to you, the franc is reckoned in gold or silver at the payer's choice; we have chosen the metal which makes us quits at the cheapest rate; the law does not forbid this."

10

It might also happen that a silver mine had been discovered in Europe, or merely that Russia were thoroughly to explore her enormous metallic veins in the Ural mountains. Should this occur, then silver would fall in price and gold would rise. Debtors, creditors, wards might well say that gold was due to them: they would be paid in silver.

It is in vain that legislators strive to maintain the two metals in equilibrium. All their efforts could have no other end than the progressive alteration of the coinage; logic and history are at one on this head, and condemn the double standard. If it be still used by several great European States, it is because modern governments avoid as much as possible meddling with monetary matters. They rightly think that the ruling power should not interfere, till the last extremity, in the exchange of things and services. But this abstention necessarily ceases on the day that a serious danger threatens private interests.

The time has come for studying an actual fact which some economists have regarded as the abandonment of a principle, but which for my part I regard as an advance towards employing gold as the sole standard. France, Italy, Switzerland, Belgium, and the Papal States have agreed to coin pieces of 20 and of 50 centimes, of 1 franc and of 2 francs of the fineness of 835 millièmes. How and why has this resolve been arrived at ? What are its immediate and remote consequences ? This is what the five governments have explained in a statement addressed to all concerned. But nations are so absent that I do not think it will be labour thrown away to explain to my readers what they are supposed to know already.

Prior to the 25th of May, 1864, fractional pieces, namely, pieces of two francs, of one franc, of 50 and of 20 centimes, were really money like the pieces of five francs. They were struck at the request of citizens (bankers or tradesmen), who found it necessary to divide their ingots into small pieces for the purposes of business. They represented an intrinsic value equal to their nominal value, except that deduction had to be made for the cost of coinage. The piece of two francs was worth two francs, less nearly two centimes; the piece of one franc was worth a little more than 99 centimes; the piece of ten sous was worth ten sous, less half a centime; the piece of four sous was worth four, less a difference which cannot be estimated in centimes.

One fine day (which was a bad day for silver money) it was perceived that the tenth part of our precious metals in the order of merit was, so to speak, withdrawn from circulation; that it left us by invisible fissures and flowed towards India, towards China, towards the regions of the far East.

This phenomenon was explicable by very natural reasons. What man is raw enough to retain his money when one comes and tells him, " Give me a thousand francs, I will return you within the hour one thousand and twenty-five? " Were you offered a thousand and five, or even a thousand and one, or a thousand francs and ten sous, you would not hesitate a moment. Everybody hastened then to exchange silver for gold, seeing that silver was at a premium. Whoever possessed savings in silver bartered them, with the premium, for a sum in gold. Exporters freighted sailing vessels, going long voyages, with our silver; ventures were made in which our pieces of five francs, of two francs, of one franc, of 50 and of 20 centimes, were carried off in the same sacks, never to return to us again.

What was the consequence? The large medal of 100 sous was not regretted, for it was gradually replaced by a small equivalent piece of gold. But the fractional pieces, starting from two francs, became conspicuous by their absence. There was a deficiency of small change. Bankers and merchants, who were accustomed to get coins struck, recognized that they played the part of dupes, for the pieces they put into circulation never returned to their coffers, and the work had always to be recommenced. They gave up sending ingots to the mint; it became almost impossible to procure fractional pieces, and the State had to interpose to lighten the public distress.

Now, is a government justified in casting several millions every year into the pitchers of the Danaides? Can it loyally perform an operation from which bankers and great merchants had withdrawn because they found it to be ruinous? No; governments are without capital; they have annual revenues, or budgets, paid by us into their hands, on the express condition that everything up to the last centime shall be expended on our behalf. Therefore they ought to abstain as scrupulously from a bad business operation as from doing a bad action. France, Italy, Switzerland, the Papal States, and Belgium, had no right to coin silver money at the expense of the public, after private persons had given up the operation because they found it ruinous.

However, it was necessary to put into our hands a measure of lower values, one less than the smallest golden coin, which was five francs. It was resolved to introduce sterling silver, of which trial had been made in England for half a century. What is this sterling? One must never have had two sous in one's pocket to be unaware of its existence. As to defining it, few men are capable of so doing in the careless and indifferent age wherein we live.

Sterling is the metallic substitute for money ; it replaces it in the smallest transactions, it accompanies it under the name of odd money in the largest ; it fills up the gaps which real money would not stop up.

The valuation of all things is made, and will be made, in real money. When the baker hands you a roll of bread worth a sou, he expects to receive in exchange 25 centigrammes of silver, 900 millièmes fine, or 16 milligrammes of gold of the same fineness. If, instead of buying one roll of bread from the same tradesman, you take 200, he will not let you have them for less than 50 grammes of silver or three grammes 2682 of lawful gold. But as it would be worse than inconvenient to reduce gold or silver to small fractions, the bread is valued in silver and paid for in copper.

Is the sou you give the baker worth the merchandise you receive in exchange ? No. The sou is a round piece of bronze, weighing five grammes. The materials of which it is composed are 95 centimes of copper, four centimes of tin, and one centime of zinc. Copper in ingots is worth from two francs to two francs 80 centimes the kilogramme, the sou's intrinsic value does not represent more than one centime when copper is two francs the kilogramme. It follows that 200 rolls would be exchangeable for

10 francs (intrinsic value) if paid for in gold or in silver, and for two francs (intrinsic value) if you bought them one by one with copper. And yet you feel yourself precisely as rich when you have five francs in sous as if you had them in gold. Why? Because bronze money, in addition to its intrinsic worth, represents a value based on social arrangement.

It has been agreed among all French citizens that a bronze sou should be given and received in all minor exchanges, and as odd money for 25 centigrammes of silver, even when it is worth five only. The Government has undertaken to manufacture, for the benefit and at the cost of the nation, this false but handy and excellent coinage. It emits as much as possible in proportion to public requirements, for if it made too much of it, the bronze coinage would be depreciated, the retailers who had it in their tills would be unable to exchange it at par, and they would consequently raise the price of their merchandise.

A very small quantity of bronze money would suffice for all the requirements of a great State which was rich and flourishing, because this instrument of exchange multiplies itself by the rapidity of its movements. Nobody is deceived as to its intrinsic value; there is thus no risk of its being withdrawn from circulation like gold and silver. Each one takes it without hesitation, as a humble tool which he will require ten times a day; but he would have lost his head were he to hoard centimes. The poor people, who add sou to sou, change their bronze for gold or silver as soon they have enough to make even money; the rich do not exchange their silver for bronze save in proportion to their wants. Everybody wishes to have a little of it, and nobody wishes to have much; bronze coin passes from one to the other, and constantly acts as a shuttlecock between the citizens of the same country. This is why a nation, possessing about six milliards in real money, does its work with sixty millions in bronze. Bronze figures in our currency for about a hundredth part only.

If you wished to dispose of these sixty millions to the foreigner, they would then be worth twelve. But they are not on sale, and no one dreams of exporting them. The French sou, in foreign parts, merely represents its intrinsic worth. Among us, and between ourselves, it has, in addition, a trust value. It is a centime of copper, with the addition of a bill of four centimes on the community of French citizens.

You may possibly ask, What profit do we find in giving and receiving sous which are worth a cent-

ime, a centime and a half, when it would be easy to
make them four or five times heavier? Copper
would then become real money like gold or silver;
40 pieces of one sou would be produced out of a
kilogramme of copper, and the trustee element would
be replaced by an increase of actual value. Yes,
but if copper became real money it would render less
service than when in the state of nominal coinage.
It would be more cumbersome, heavier, and almost
painful to employ. The law allows a debtor to pay
up to five francs in bronze; this is half a kilogramme
to carry. It would amount to two kilogrammes and
a half if the metal were given and received at its
intrinsic value. Besides, the price of copper constantly changes; it would be necessary to re-cast
the sou several times in the year. Now, the cost of
manufacture is almost as great as the metal itself.
Lastly, if it be impossible, or at least very difficult,
to get on with two standards, the time is unpro-
pitious for adding a third.

Our epoch thinks so little of raising copper to the
rank of money that it has caused silver to descend to
the humble level of bronze coinage. This is the best
and the only way to preserve the fractional pieces of
which small traders have so much want every day.
The bronze coinage is well guarded against flowing
away, seeing that it loses four-fifths of its value in

crossing the frontier.   Our 60 millions of sous and
of centimes will assuredly remain among us until
they shall be worn out, and as they have been cut
out of a solid material, we shall not require to re-melt
them for a long time.

The new fractional pieces which have begun to
circulate are equally guaranteed against the exportation which periodically sweeps over us.   Nobody
would gain by exporting them to China, nobody is
interested in melting them into ingots, because their
intrinsic worth is below their nominal value.   The
speculator who was so badly advised as to withdraw
them from circulation could only lose by so doing.

One thousand kilogrammes coined at the rate of
900 millièmes of fineness would represent 900 kilogrammes of pure silver; 1000 kilogrammes of the
new money would not contain more than 850 kilogrammes of fine silver.   The minimum difference
is 65 kilogrammes.   Therefore, if the fancy should
strike you to collect 200,000 pieces of one franc,
entirely new, to cast them into the melting-pot, this
trifling operation would cost you 65 kilogrammes of
pure silver, at 218 francs 89 centimes the kilogramme,
or 14,227 francs 85 centimes, without counting the
laboratory expenses and other small outgoings.
Therefore, 200,000 francs in real money, for instance,
in large pieces of a hundred francs, would be worth

about 1400 francs more than 200,000 francs in alloyed coin. Therefore, 20 francs of the old money are worth 1 franc 40 centimes more than the new substitute for money; he who exchanges a five-franc piece in gold or silver for fractional pieces receives about 35 centimes less than he has given.

But what does it matter? I lose seven sous every time I exchange five francs, but the 93 sous which remain over are accepted as five francs in my own country, at Rome, in Belgium, in Switzerland, and in Italy. Five new one-franc pieces are worth 4 francs 65 centimes, plus 35 centimes guaranteed by the nation.

It is the State which issues and guarantees the alloyed silver; it undertakes to accept it, at the rate of issue, at all the public offices, whatever be the amount of the sum paid in. In private transactions, the law decrees that this alloyed silver shall serve for small payments only, it is not legally current among us for more than twenty francs.

These arrangements openly made and brought to the knowledge of everybody, will accustom the people to consolidate their savings in gold specie, and to consider silver as a simple instrument of exchange. It will no longer be classed with things to be hoarded; no longer will small pieces be collected to the detriment of commerce. Note particularly that this quasi money of 835 degrees of fineness still contains a respectable proportion of real value, since out of a thousand kilogrammes it contains 835 of pure metal. This is nearly the alloy of second-rate silver ware (840) ; it is 85 millièmes more than third-rate silver ; no matter. It is enough that its conventional value should be slightly greater than its intrinsic value, in order that the hoarder and the gambler should not meddle with it, and that it should be entirely left to - its proper use, that is, to circulate.

It is not necessary to be a sorcerer to predict the effects of this minor monetary revolution ; it is sufficient to observe what takes place across the Channel. The English, who are our masters in social economy, have selected gold as the sole standard. Their smallest piece of real money is worth about 12 francs 50 centimes. For purposes of giving change and making small payments, they have two kinds of alloyed coin ; sterling silver of the magnificent standard of 925, but lighter in weight, and quoted sensibly above its intrinsic value ; alloyed copper coins, less handy and less beautiful than ours, nearly twice as heavy, but of which the intrinsic value does not attain to a half of the nominal value. With these elements, an absolute measure of value and two approximative measures, conventionally admitted in the interests of commerce, England pro-

duces, exchanges, saves more than any country in
the world; add to this that she does twice or thrice
more business, while employing two or three times
less currency, than we do.

The compass of this study and its special destina-
tion prevent me from enlarging on the ingenious
machinery by the aid of which a civilized people
performs numerous transactions with a small amount
of money. The current account, the cheque, the bill
of exchange, the bank note, and many other wonders
of financial industry, only slightly interest, and
rightly so, the great majority of workers. What
come home to them are wages, savings, capital, revenue, association, co-operation; let us discuss them.

Merely permit me to end this chapter with a patriotic reflection.

We see that three independent, enlightened, and
hard-working nations have adopted our currency
and the final consequence of the metric system.
Henceforth 70 millions of Europeans will speak
the same language every time that lengths, surfaces, quantities, weights, and values are in question.
Will the metric system halt after having gone so
far? I am sure that it will gain the suffrages of
every nation one after the other. Some countries have
rejected it till now for two reasons. The first, purely
theoretical, is that one of our scientific men (Méchain)

made a slight error in his measurement of the meridian. The second, more practical, is the utopia of the double standard, so unfortunately adopted by our legislators of the year XI.

By adopting at last a single standard, we shall get rid of the only serious objection which the metric system has encountered in its course; it has been said that the great American nation is about to assimilate its gold coinage to ours. After doing so, how can it reject our metre, our litre, our kilogramme, which are logical in another way than our 20-franc piece? The French idea is destined to conquer the civilized world, and this victory will be worth any other, though it shall not have cost a drop of blood.

CHAPTER VIII.

WAGES.

WHEN I recall my college teachings, I find that wages are the payment for a service. We were told, in those days, that this word (*salaire*) had the same etymology as salad. *Sal*, in Latin, denotes a condiment which is indispensable to man, that is, salt. I do not require to inform you what relation there is between salt, or *sal*, and the green and salted vegetable which composes our salad. Between salt, or *sal*, and wages, the connection is less evident at Paris. But in Abyssinia, at the moment I write, salt is used as money; tradition records that it constituted the payment of free labourers at the foundation of Rome. The citizen who had worked for another said to him, " Give me my salt," as others now say, " Give me my money." Salt being regarded as the synonyme for money, to give a wage and to pay are one and the same thing.

It is eternally just that a free man, after having toiled for a year, for a month, for a day, or for an hour to the profit of another man, should receive the equivalent of the services he has rendered.

You know that to work for nothing is to work like a slave. We affirm our independence every time that we say to our equal, "I have served you; it is your turn now." Not only is there no shame in demanding the price of the labour we have performed, but he among us who should suffer himself to be used as a tool without claiming reciprocity, would descend to the level of an ox or of a horse.

Therefore, to assimilate wage-paid labour to servile labour is to represent the exact opposite of the truth. This definition, though common enough in the streets, is absurd for two reasons; in the first place, because wages are the opposite of labour; in the second, because the slave is the only man who works without receiving wages.

But perhaps it may seem to you that I employ the word in too general a sense. I am rather inclined to think that a certain school has too greatly limited its meaning for some years back. We have witnessed the birth and growth of that fantastic monster, the scapegoat of modern society, which people have begun to stone under the name of the wages-class. Recently, whilst reading a very eloquent tirade on the humiliating oppression of wages, I got from Paris an assignation or summons (I am not sure which, but it was a paper) calling upon me to give evidence in a Court of Justice. On the back of the paper I read this printed form, which was consequently not addressed to me only, " the witness will receive his wage."

Did not that supply food for reflection? Every year our Judges address the same invitation, couched in the same terms, to half a million of Frenchmen, if not more. I should suppose that three-fourths of my fellow-citizens receive a document of the like kind at least once in their lives. Now, it is impossible that the law, that lofty expression of public wisdom, should deliberately insult nearly the whole of the nation. If wage implies a meaning which is insulting, or even disagreeable, care would have been taken not to associate it with men who are summoned to give evidence on oath. Evidently, the public authorities interpret this word in the same sense as the greatest legislators of the world of antiquity. They say, " If we give a man trouble, we confiscate his day to the profit of the general interest, the community owes him something in return ; he shall receive salt or money wherewith to buy it, a product, a thing, a wage."

Now there is but one justice, one morality, one

truth in the world. The man who renders a service to another ought to be recompensed in return. In every partially civilized society, the individual produces day by day a certain sum of things which are thrown into general consumption, and which return to him under the form of wages. We live by that only. My neighbour in the country is a farmer who grows, one year with another, 1000 hectolitres of corn. When he carries his crops to market, consumers, coming from all quarters, take away his products wherewith to feed themselves, giving him in ex-change 30,000 francs; this is a fine figure. But the farmer has to pay wages; so much to the landlord who has leased him a piece of cleared land and suit-able farm-buildings; so much to the money-lender who has let him have the wherewithal to purchase oxen, horses, ploughs, corn-seed; so much to the helpers who have worked under his direction; so much to the great political machine which guarantees his security. When he shall have paid all the wages he owes, there will be four or five hundred francs over, representing the wage of his yearly toil. This sum is certainly his; no other person has any claim to it; he is its sole master and rightful owner; he is entitled to use and abuse it, that is, to consume it till nothing remains, if such be his pleasure.

My other neighbour is a large manufacturer who

disposes of several millions' worth of wrought-iron annually. He harvests, instead of corn, files, tools, crinoline steels, works more or less ingenious, more or less useful, but all in general demand in the markets of Europe. In proportion to the extent of his sales he pockets a large sum, four millions at least, which are paid to him by a hundred wholesale traders. But he is himself a debtor for several millions of wages. The capital, or the immense instrument he sets in motion, belongs to the two hundred persons who lend it him; he must pay these persons wages. The five or six hundred men who forge, chisel, file, fit, and polish articles in his different workshops, are not slaves bound down to labour; they come to the factory because they choose to do so; each of them makes his terms beforehand and stipulates as to his wages. When everybody has been paid what he is entitled to, the head of the factory will make his calculations, and say, "Everything having been taken into account, my own wage is so much. Last year it was 100,000 francs; the year previously 12,000; sometimes it is nil; sometimes it is less than nothing, that is a notable enough loss, for everything is not profit in industrial pursuits, no more is it in commerce, nor even in agriculture. There are years when one considers he is fortunate in having made both ends meet, and in avoiding the sadly negative form of wage which is called bankruptcy."

When you enter a grocer's shop to get half a kilogramme of sugar, the 75 centimes you throw upon the counter are not the shopkeeper's wage alone; the sum has to be divided between several thousand of individuals who have directly or indirectly contributed to the service which this pound of sugar will render to you. Your business is with the tradesman; he asks a price which he knows, or considers, to be remunerative. He has made his calculation beforehand; he has proved to himself that if he were to sell his sugar for 75 centimes, he will be able to pay all the wages of the other producers and take one centime or two as his own wage. It may be that he is mistaken; perhaps, on balancing his accounts at the end of the year, he will perceive that his calculations were wrong, that the total amount of these wages reduces the sum to zero, or even that he has lost more than he had earned. That is his business. In your case, once the merchandise has been paid for, you have nothing to do with the seller. Happen what will, you and he are quits. Should he come, two years afterwards, and tell you, " I have become bankrupt, experience has shown me that I ought to have sold my sugar a sou dearer," you will reply to him, " So much the worse for you." If, on the other hand, you should meet him ten years afterwards in a two-horse carriage, you would not be justified in saying to him that he had sold his sugar a sou too dear and pocketed an exorbitant wage. He has carried on business at his risk and peril; so much the better for him, should he have grown rich.

Every transaction ought to be upright. If the grocer should give you plaster or flour instead of sugar, he robs you; if he should deliver to you 450 grammes instead of 500, he robs you. If you pay him in bad money, you rob him; if you do not pay him at all, you are a thief. But once you have received true weight and genuine articles and have paid in real money the price freely agreed upon, you have nothing more to settle with the tradesman, neither has he anything to settle with you. It concerns him to clear up his accounts and to extract his wages from them, if he can.

The manufacturer, the tradesman, and, in general, all who work at their own risk and peril, are tossed about between hope and fear. They all dream of realizing a large profit which will repay them for their toil, but they also know that possibly they are working for nothing. The destiny of business is so capricious that an intelligent and upright man may ruin himself by his labours, may lose in six months the fruits of twenty years of exertion, his patrimony, his reputation for honesty, everything, in short, save life and liberty. Hence it is, so to speak, that an instinct of legitimate defence inclines him to sell everything as dear as possible, to buy everything as cheaply as possible. The counterpoise to this tendency lies in the energy of the opposite party. The consumer defends himself against the exorbitant demand of the seller; he goes to the cheapest market, giving the preference to the tradesman who contents himself with the lowest wage. The small producer defends himself in turn against the avarice of contractors. He puts himself up to auction, selling his services to the highest bidder. The result of all these movements, in an opposite sense, is an unstable equilibrium; industrial liberty has its fluctuations like the ocean, and sometimes its tempests. Now, everybody has not got sea legs. Should the spirit of adventure and a robust constitution lead several thousands of persons to double the Cape of Good Hope, there are millions who prefer solid land to the finest steamer buffeted by the gale.

In proportion as society becomes settled, we perceive an increase in the prudent multitude of unambitious labourers who prefer certainty to chance. Long before actuaries had produced the great conception of "Assurance by division of risks," one knew

how to assure oneself individually against the
element of chance which always renders the recom-
pense of labour doubtful. When a man has learned
by ten years of experience that his average wages
are 1500 francs, he estimates himself at his industrial value and says, "I am a man of 1500 francs a
year. If I labour on my own account my total
profits or wages would amount in good years, perhaps,
to 3000 francs, but it is also possible that in a bad
year I should earn absolutely nothing. Upon what,
then, shall I live? On the savings I have made in
advance. But if the bad precedes the good year I
shall not have a centime in hand; must I then die of
hunger? Let me first assure my existence."

It is, therefore, the instinct of preservation which
leads many persons to prefer a small fixed salary to
a large uncertain income.

The shopman sells his services to his employer
for so much a month. He knows that if he were to
set up on his own account he would probably turn
his intelligence and activity to more profitable account;
that perhaps he would earn twice, ten times, twenty
times as much. But in the first place he has neither
the capital nor the credit requisite for founding the
most humble establishment. Moreover, he is intimately acquainted with the difficulties, the risks, the
dangers of commerce, and he deems himself fortunate

in escaping from all initiative and all responsibility. Whether the balance at the end of the year be on the right or the wrong side, he receives his monthly pay. Should his employer become bankrupt, his own hands are clean.

The artificer does not earn as much as his master or even the humblest shophand ; but he does not put in any capital, he risks nothing ; when he has finished his task or ended his day he knows that he has earned four or five francs or upwards ; he dines and sleeps devoid of care. Perhaps, however, the product of his labour will be sold at a loss or rejected by the consumer, that is to say, buried altogether, raw material, labour, and all. So much the worse for the master. The artificer does not enter into these details. He has contributed his labour, received his pay ; he has no further concern about the eventual products of the business ; his contract is formal, and in case of misfortune no one can demand a centime from him.

Medical men, advocates, solicitors, notaries, ushers, stock-brokers, produce-brokers, bankers, all work in view of an uncertain wage. Whether called honorarium, brokerage, commission, premium, matters nothing; it is always a wage, the payment for a service.

Minor and important public functionaries all enjoy a fixed wage, which bears diverse names, but which in no respect differs from the wage received by a shopman or journeyman labourer. The pay of a gamekeeper, the fees of a schoolmaster, the legacy of an executor, the salary of a bishop, of a rector, of a professor, of a prefect, of a minister, the pay of a marshal of France, the pay of a senator, the sovereign's civil list, are wages, wages, wages ! In a Republican State, the president is chief among all who receive wages; in a monarchy the chief wage-receiver is the emperor or the king. Wages are not then humiliating in themselves, since a man's highest ambition is to figure in the Budget for the largest sum.

Oh, then everybody receives wages, except the man who lives on his dividends? I do not except him even. Dividends are always paid by some one, are they not? And no one pays them for pleasure, but in exchange for a service. The farmer recompenses the service rendered in intrusting him with some hectares of land. The rent is then the wages of the landed proprietor.

A tenant pays four times a year for the humble or sumptuous shelter which another man accords to him; each quarter's rent is a wage obtained by the proprietor of the house.

The manufacturer and the merchant who work with other people's money pay wages to the capitalist who acts as sleeping partner.

11

The traveller who takes his ticket at a railway station pays wages to the contractors who provide means of transport, that is, to you, to me, to all those who have a railway share in our possession.

The State, or the community of citizens, pays wages four times yearly to all those who have advanced money to it, whether for the expenses of war or for works of peace. State bonds, shares, debentures, debts in writing or mortgages, city houses, lands, everything which yields interest or rent, represent a service rendered and rendered for a wage. All of us are paid and pay wages, for civilized life is a perpetual exchange of services.

CHAPTER IX.

THE population of the terrestrial globe, according to the most recent calculations, is about 1,350,000,000 of men. Suppose the average production of labour to be one franc per head, and the average consumption one franc. At the end of one century, or of fifty centuries, the human race would be at the same point as at present. It would require the same amount of effort to produce the same quantity of useful things and to satisfy the same wants. An unexpected occurrence, an accident, a misfortune, would find posterity as helpless as their forefathers; each time a plague were to destroy one hundred thousand daily rations, one hundred thousand persons would fast for a day. The slightest interruption of labour would bring about famine, and if the interruption lasted a short time, people would perish in thousands. This is no mere hypothesis. All the races which have persisted in living from ' hand to mouth have finally become extinct, whatever might be the richness of their native country and the geniality of its climate.

Suppose on the other hand that all living beings were to agree to save the tenth of their income, that is, two sous daily, on an average. The general account would exhibit a return of 135 millions the first evening, 49 milliards 275 millions at the end of the year, 4 trillions 927 milliards 500 millions at the end of the first century. And what is a century in the life of the human race? Hardly as much as one day in the life of a man.

A daily saving of two sous per head would thus constitute a capital of 3650 francs for each person in a hundred years, if we were to content ourselves with laying up treasure like illiterate peasants or half-savage nations. But, if the human race were to lay its savings out at interest in proportion as they were realized, the result would be still more imposing. You know that 1000 francs invested at five per cent. yield 131,000 francs in a century, and 16 millions 768 thousand francs in two centuries.

Now, what would happen if the community of men were but ten times richer than at present? The working day might be reduced from ten hours to one only; or rather, he who should work ten hours would procure ten times more things in exchange for his labour.

Strictly speaking, you have the right to consume from day to day all that you have produced, but reasoning and experience prove to you that the fruits of your labour, when accumulated in savings, become the instruments of easier and more lucrative labour. There was a time when the man who wished to remove a heap of sand, scraped the sand with his nails, and carried it away piecemeal in his two hands. Such was the infancy of industry,—labour prior to the creation of capital. The day that this primitive navvy either learned to save the time to make a pick and a basket, or had the power of obtaining them through the medium of exchange, he was better armed against nature. This small capital, wretched as it may appear to you, enables him to do more work with less exertion, and to earn a better day's wage. Should he persevere in saving, he will exchange his basket for a wheel-barrow, which is a still more lucrative capital. The wheel-barrow is succeeded by the cart, and progress does not stop there. When you see fifty trucks filled with ballast running along a railway, they are drawn by a large capital, one which performs in an hour the work which two hundred thousand hands could not accomplish in a year.

The first spinners twisted the thread with their fingers, without any other instrument. I leave you to imagine how much they would earn at that occupation. Yet the day came when one of these poor wretches saved the price of a spindle out of her earnings. A spindle was a small capital, which facilitated work and brought in a return. Out of the humble profits of the spindle, protracted economy got enough wherewith to buy a spinning-wheel. And later, when saving had created a large capital, you may see, in England alone, 30 millions of spindles turning of their own accord, and producing more thread in a day than all the spinners in the world could twist in ten years with their fingers. Now, only 451,000 persons are required to watch these 30 millions of spindles, therefore each worker, man, woman, or child, manages 66 on an average. And if you take into account the giddy rapidity of this labour and its fairylike perfection, you will perceive that the daily production of the individual is not merely multiplied by 66, but is several hundred times multiplied, thanks to capital.

Let two men of the same strength work with equal assiduity during the same number of hours, the product of the first will be as 1 and of the second as 1000, if the first merely uses his hands and the other a perfect system of machinery. Now, machinery is a capital formed by individual or collective saving. Nature has not supplied capital; it has been wholly created by man for his personal use.

A city is nothing but an accumulation of capital. The pavement of the streets, the sewers, the quays, the apparatus for lighting, represent capitalized savings (which are placed at the service of future labour) by several generations of men. These are the instruments of security, of salubrity, of rapid communication, without which labour languishes. Closed and covered houses are capital for lack of which labour would be paralyzed by cold, by heat, by the inclemency of the weather. In all workshops, in all shops, in all strong boxes, you meet with stationary or floating capital, machines, tools, arms for sport or for war, raw and wrought metals, furnishings of all kinds, reserves of gold and of silver which daily furnish the advances necessary for labour.

The country abounds with capital like the city, in a civilized land. Highways, roads, canals, dykes, houses, huts, flocks grazing, ponds stocked with fish, cleared fields, grafted trees, and I know not what. This animal, harnessed to a cart, is one capital drawing another.

But if the smallest instrument of labour be capital, then all men are capitalists? Yes, nearly all, but in frightfully unequal proportions. Between the rag-picker, who possesses implements worth six francs, and the banker, who has a hundred millions at his disposal, the inequality is startling. We ought to deplore these contrasts; we ought to deplore them all the more because too great an inequality in the distribution of riches arrests the increase of the population. In society, it is necessary to have a large capital at command; this is necessary in the working man's own interest, in order that he may be paid for his daily toil. If the mason who works at the foundation of a house, if the labourer who sows corn, had to live on credit, the one till harvest-time, the other till the building was fitted for occupation, both of them would have all that time during which to die of hunger. They exist, thanks to some large capital out of which their daily bread is given to them. But, on the other hand, it is easy to understand why the population tends to decrease in countries where the disproportion between fortunes is enormous. The individual who alone holds ten millions has no need to increase his wealth; he only thinks about investing it as safely as possible and enjoying the interest. His capital, invested at four or five per cent., will yield him an income of four or five millions. No one man can expend so much money without lavishing much of it: the lesser portion of his income will be usefully employed; the larger will flow away in unproductive expenditure. And whilst an individual squanders, without profit to human society, what would support two or three thousand families, those who possess a capital of six francs, like the ragpicker and many others, will produce arduously and little, for want of proper tools; they will barely consume what is absolutely necessary; they will dread the burden of a wife and children, whom they are not able to support. I admit that this a hundred-fold millionnaire begets as many sons and daughters as nature will grant him: even when he shall have twelve children (which is hardly customary among the rich), these little ladies and these little gentlemen will cause an enormous injury to society; they will cost it several thousands of plebeians, whom the largeness of their patrimony has prevented from being born.

Suppose that the hundred millions of Mr X. or of Mr Z. were divided into five thousand portions of twenty thousand francs each. Twenty thousand francs are not a large capital, but they constitute an instrument of a certain power. The man who possesses twenty thousand francs obtains without too great difficulty, if he be honest, credit to the extent of thirty thousand; he is not rich enough to live with folded arms, but he has the means for labouring advantageously. He can think about marrying, obtain a woman's hand, and give himself the luxury of being a parent. The capital enables him to beget a family; the family feeling induces him to save, and saving augments his capital.

In all probability, this humble worker will leave behind him, on earth, a patrimony which he has enlarged, and two or three children whom he has reared. He will thus have contributed to progress, added something to the general inventory, which is made up of realized property and intelligent forces.

The very rich man does not save because he has no need so to do; the very poor man does not save because he barely earns enough to exist upon ; if perchance he has a few francs in his pocket, he is inclined to expend them in excesses, for if he put them aside he would not be sensibly poorer. If you preach economy to him, he will reply, "What is the good of it? It is not worth the trouble?" It is not necessary to advise the small capitalist to save; he does so by instinct, and teaches his children to save by his example.

It were desirable, then, in the interest of the human race, that the distribution of riches was less unequal, and that every individual at the age he is able to work should have at hand, so to speak, an instrument of useful labour. Well-meaning men unite in saying that the world would go on better if this were the case. But to desire and to obtain are very different things; this is the obstacle. The right of property is absolute. When a fisherman has remained a whole day on a river's bank to catch half-a-dozen fish, his catch belongs to him as indisputably as his head, his arm, or his leg. He is quite knocked up, that is, he has exchanged a part of his body for these fish; he alone has the right to eat the fish to recruit his strength; the product of his toil proceeds from him, and ought to return to him alone. When evening comes, if this worthy fellow be wise enough to think of the morrow, frugal enough to leave off with an appetite, if he eat but five fish out of six, and if he put by the sixth, he is clearly entitled to do so; the fish he keeps will belong to him to-morrow as absolutely as to-day. Should he prefer to sell it for two sous rather than to keep it, and if he put the two sous into a money-box, are the two sous less his own than the fish? No. And, when the money-box is full, should he open it and find a hundred francs, these hundred francs will belong to him as unquestionably as each piece of two sous belonged to him separately. This is not in virtue of a formal law, it is in virtue of the natural law which written laws only embody and sanction, but which under no pretext can they abrogate.

He who has saved up a hundred francs is free to do with them what he pleases, provided he does not use them to another's detriment. He might eat them at a single meal in the Café Anglais ; he would have swallowed in the course of the evening a thousand fish at two sous each, but no one would have the right to interfere. He might throw them into the river ; to do so would be equivalent to burying a thousand fish in a large hole ; he would act foolishly, yet he would have the right to do it. He might exchange the money for a net, which would be a useful capital. The hundred francs thus transformed would become his helpers ; thanks to them, he would catch more fish in a shorter time, and with less fatigue.

If another, who fished with a line, were to say to him, " Lend me your net to-day, and I will give you the half of what I catch," he would render service for service, according to the great natural law of reciprocity. The borrower counts upon taking at least three times more fish with the net than with a line, otherwise he would not have come and made the bargain. If he be not mistaken in his expectations, he will still get a profit after paying for the service rendered.

Suppose that at the moment he opened his money-box, when the hundred francs, carefully counted over, were displayed on a table, and the small capitalist meditated as to how he should use them, and a neighbour came and said to him, " Lend me your money, I will return it next year." The lawful possessor would reply, " This money is the fruit of my saving ; I did not collect it except by enduring privations, I would not have stinted myself, unless I had some enjoyment in prospect. I count upon exchanging it for a net, or for some other improved instrument, which will render my labour more lucrative and less hard. Wherefore should I make over to you a benefit which I acquired at the cost of much exertion ? Wherefore should I add the additional value to your labour which has been honestly acquired for mine ? If I hand over to you the profit of my toil and privations, you must give me something in return." " But," replies the borrower, " your money will not breed young." " No, if it were left in a drawer ; moreover no one borrows for the foolish pleasure of hoarding. But you would go and purchase with my money a second pair of arms which would work for you. You would fish more profitably, thanks to me ; therefore you owe me a portion of the earnings I enable you to get." In virtue of these reasons, which are irrefutable, the borrower of the hundred francs promises to return a hundred and five at the end of the year. Do these hundred and five francs lawfully belong to the lender? Is he their absolute master? Is he at liberty to consume the interest of his small capital? And if he forego the pleasure of consuming it, if he put it by, is he free to re-invest capital and interest, to render a greater service for a larger return, to pocket a year later a hundred and ten francs twenty-five centimes? And if this man lives long enough in order, by dint of working, saving, and lending, to realize the sum of one thousand francs, is not he the only person in the world who has any claim to this capital? Should it please him to swallow it at a . mouthful, the human race would have nothing to say, any more than if he had eaten the sixth fish on the day the notion of saving first entered his mind. For a stronger reason is he entitled to dispose of his property, whether by gift or will, and to bequeath to his son or to a friend, the instrument of labour which has been the work of his lifetime?

The donee or the heir, if he follow the same course, might be able to leave ten thousand francs to his son, who later might leave one hundred thousand. In proportion as the survivors are better furnished with tools, they will have the better chance of creating a large capital.

A large capital has, then, the same origin and the same inviolable character as a small one. The banker's hundred millions are as sacred as the peasant's cow and the navvy's pick; the selfsame principle, anterior and superior to all formal laws, protects the one and the other. To lay hands on capital is to attack the human body in its closest incarnation. It is as monstrous to strip a man of his savings as to reduce him to slavery. In fact, slavery is the confiscation of potential labour; the other crime is the confiscation of labour performed.

Some crooked spirits pay court to working men by affirming that chance and violence have created and distributed capital. Chance, they say, has disposed of the earth to the first comer, war and conquest have introduced our landlords by force; the accident of birth summonses some children to share millions, while the disinherited millions die of hunger.

The truth on these three heads is as follows. One must be very ignorant of the origin of our species to suppose that the first man had only to take possession of fruitful domains. The primeval earth is no capital, any more than the wild or ferocious animals which inhabit it. Centuries of labour have been required to clear, drain, and properly prepare the fields which at the present day are worth two or three thousand francs the hectare, and were worth less than nothing at the outset; above all, prodigies of courage were required to dispossess the prior holders of our country. They were the bear, the hyena, and the lion of the caves, the mammoth elephant and the woolly rhinoceros. The geologist finds the bones of these monsters heaped indiscriminately with those of our poor ancestors, those first occupants who are represented to us as the spoiled children of capital and the sybarites of landed property.

It is true that, during a long series of ages, brute force often installed the conqueror in the place of the conquered. Lands, houses, flocks, gold and silver, have been a hundred times taken and retaken. The caprice of kings, the favour of the great, intrigues, fraud, confiscations, have ravished more than one capital from its honest creator to hand it over to others. But goods wrongfully acquired merely pass through the hands of the evil-doer; they quickly return to the general mass, and capital and savings re-acquire them with little noise. We all know how one becomes a landlord in the year of grace 1872. One creates a capital by dint of toil and saving, and one exchanges the whole or a part for a landed property. Not an inch of French soil has been otherwise obtained; not a landlord's title is based on occupation or conquest. In our day those who possess a bit of land have created its equivalent, they have extracted it from themselves, so to speak; at least, they have obtained it by inheritance.

It is not by chance that a son is his father's heir. His patrimony and his birth spring from the same source; the same man calls him into existence and collects for him wherewithal to live. Assuredly, the father would have produced and saved less, had he no one to provide for. Thus, the son is at least the occasional cause of the fortune he pockets.

The working men are told that they are disinherited; nothing is more false. Disinherited by whom? Disinherited of what? Their fathers have left nothing to them. Do they pretend to be the heirs of a person to whom they are unknown, to the detriment of the legitimate successors? "But the earth was divided without us, and our lot has not been reserved." And how could your birth be foreseen? Had this been done, had there been retained for you a hectare and 40 ares per head (which is very nearly what you would have got), what would you do with a piece of untilled land, with no capital to render it valuable? Land in itself is not wealth before labour has been expended on it; it is but a source of expense. And if you succeed by a miracle in clearing your patch, would you think it pleasant, on the day you were beginning to reap the harvest of your toil, if one came and said to you, "Give back ten ares; two millions having been added to the population, provision must be made for the new comers " ?

Besides, it is not true that the land has been entirely taken up., The soil of France has indeed been appropriated, because we are a large nation condensed in a narrow space; but three days' journey from here, in Algeria, there are millions of hectares to be obtained. Men are deficient in Brazil, in Egypt, in the United States, and land superabounds there. If man struggling with primeval · soil could gain his end without capital, I know ten governments who would quickly summon you, and would pay your passage across the sea. On the other side of the ocean, the emigrant is in great demand. North America welcomes, one year with another, 300,000 workers born and bred in Europe, at the expense of Europe, who have cost, one with the other, twelve thousand francs to our old exhausted land : it is estimated that about ten thousand francs are required to make a man. This is an annual tax of three milliards which the New World levies on the Old. Yet even when you have the offer of a free passage to the Far West, and a gift of 20 hectares per head there, I do not advise you to close with it : it is less dangerous to walk unarmed against a tiger than to clear a virgin soil without capital.

CHAPTER X.

Poor people who work and suffer, if a man should tell you that everything is for the best in the best of worlds, raise the hue and cry upon the optimist. But, if another comes and says to you that the malady of the working classes can be cured in a few days or even in a few years, be on your guard against the impostor.

In order that John, Peter, or Paul, on arriving at adult age should find within their reach a complete and perfect tool (that is, capital), it is not enough that capital should abound in society ; it is still essential that a relation, a benefactor, a providence in human shape, should have taken care to provide capital with a view of keeping John, Peter, or Paul. There is no combination which can supply the foresight of ancestors where, unhappily, it is wanting.

The worker without capital, or working man, is

obliged to hire the tools which belong to another man and to pay for their hire out of his wages. This necessity diminishes his earnings by one half, by the fourth part, sometimes by the tenth, of what he would obtain were he to employ his own capital. Such is the case of the small retail dealer who borrows one thousand francs to establish himself, and of the artificer who borrows from his master a machine worth several millions, in order to earn three francs a day.

In all circumstances, the workman considers he is robbed because he exaggerates the value of his labour and depreciates the value of capital, his co-operator. Frequently, even, he thinks he is killed by the capitalist, and this error is chiefly common among the most civilized workmen. As his wants are more numerous than those of a day labourer or a peasant, he is more hard to satisfy, and, in all sincerity, he considers himself in want of necessaries when he earns two or three times more than a ploughboy. He exclaims, with perfect good faith, that his throat is being cut, that his masters are eating his flesh and drinking his blood. Raise as an objection the law of supply and demand, he will deny it and reply by a metaphor about the living instrument: "I am a living instrument; he who makes use of me must first support, repair, and keep me clean and shining." It is perfectly impossible to found concord on such a basis, for man's wants are illimitable; one succeeds the other.

There was a time when ambitious persons turned to account the discontent of working men. They were induced to make revolutions; they were told, give us power and we will give you comfort.

But the strongest, the most despotic government, could not in any wise modify the relations between labour and capital. Were the working men to be in the majority in a country, were they to employ universal suffrage to place a working man on the throne, were they to have a Legislative Assembly, an administration, and courts of justice exclusively composed of working men, they would not succeed in altering the distribution of wealth, or even in obtaining five centimes increase in their daily wages. For the right of property is placed upon a height inaccessible to all political decrees; the law itself cannot interfere with it save under the penalty of ceasing to be law. If the majority of the citizens voted for the spoliation of a single person, they would but perpetrate a solemn act of brigandage. May the State itself interpose between working men and capitalists in order to lend to one the money of the other? Not at all. If the capitalist knows the working man sufficiently well to intrust him with his property on a personal guaranty, he will spontaneously lend it to him without the in-

tervention of the State.   If he have good reasons, or
even bad ones, for retaining the free disposition of his
money, the State cannot violate an absolute right
without committing a crime.   As for the intervention of authority in fixing the tariff of wages, it
springs from absurdity and returns to absurdity.   A
man cannot be compelled to pay a service at a price
higher than that at which he rates it.   Contractors
purchase the labourer's service to dispose of it at a
profit; if you put them in a position to give so
high a price that they must experience a loss in dis-
posing of it, they will not purchase it again.   Therefore, to abolish the law of supply and demand would
be as ingenious as to cancel the law of gravitation, or
to decree that in the future two and two should make
five.

All the efforts made till now to organize labour
arbitrarily, have only served to frighten capital, to
impede production, to diminish consumption, and to
impose a cruel fast upon working men.   Do they
accept the experiment as decisive?   It is said they
do, and I am pleased to think so.

The Second Empire owed them much, and spared
no pains to preserve their sympathies.   Long ago,
it is credibly said, the Empire would have undertaken the levelling of riches, if the absolute power
of a man could effect the result.   But, being convinced

that authority could do nothing between capital and labour, this strong government, attached to its power, spontaneously relinquished the attempt. It bound its hands in presence of the great battle of economic interests, in order that capital and labour might freely settle their scores.

Scarcely had the liberty of association been proclaimed when the Paris workmen wished to try a strike. This was a new experiment, which I followed with sustained attention and sorrowful interest.

A strike starts from the principle that industrial capital has need of the day labourer as the day labourer has need of it. The workmen arrive at a common understanding and say to the contractors, "If you do not raise our wages, we will fold our arms, production will cease, your capital will no longer yield anything, your credit will expire, your customers will leave you, and you will be ruined." The masters are now greatly troubled. At the time a strike begins their hands are full of orders, their products have been sold beforehand deliverable at a certain date, at a fixed price, and the price is based on the labourer's old scale of wages. In general, thanks to competition, the margin is not large between the selling price and the amount which is returned. If the law laid down by the working men be obeyed, goods must be manufactured at a loss which may end in ruin. If it be a question who is to go to the wall, the manufacturers possessing courage prefer having recourse to extreme measures; they suspend business and oppose the idleness of capital to the idleness of the arms. National production is stopped; consumption is restricted, or supplies are procured from abroad. This crisis lasts a few weeks, after which the working men and the masters, having been sorely tried, come to an amicable arrangement, and they end where they should have begun. But on the morrow of such a shock, the resumption of work always takes place under sad conditions. A leaven of rancour remains at the bottom of all hearts; capital and labour are only reconciled under compulsion; the remembrance of hostilities will long survive.

That is not all. The working men have carried on war at their own expense and at the cost of their families. They have borne privations; they have witnessed, they have caused, the sufferings of their wives and children; strength, health, gaiety, household harmony have received some shocks; there is less heart for work. The small sum of money laid by, the humble treasure representing the savings of years, has vanished in a few days; one has even run into debt for a time. I should like to think that so many sacrifices have not been thrown away, and that the strike has caused a certain proportionate rise

in wages. But, if the hour in the workshop be paid
a few centimes additional, it will appear twice as long
and more tiresome to the man who pockets but
a portion of his wages and who works to pay off his
debts.

And if strikes have killed industry, who enables
you to live? What if the consumer, discommoded in
his habits or annoyed by your demands, should strike
in turn and dispense with your products? That has
occurred: I have examples at the tip of my pen.
Without going so far, what if the public, which
enables you to live, should henceforth give its orders
to foreign manufacturers? There is no longer any
law which compels French consumers to make their
purchases in France. Very recently, the strike of the
Parisian hatters caused a large importation of English hats, the strike of the Parisian coach-builders
caused fine orders to be sent to the Brussels manufacturers.

The weak side of a strike has not escaped the
notice of the principal leaders of the working men,
who, I admit, are eminent strategists. For three or
four years one has seen the germs of a working-
class league co-extensive with the civilized world.
Nothing less is aimed at than to unite together all
those who work with their hands, in Europe and
America, to obtain a rise in wages everywhere simul-

12

tancously. A great council, the true government of the universal working-class, would decree and maintain a strike wherever it appeared to be useful or just. If this grandiose plan were carried into execution, neither the contractors nor the consumers of Paris would be able to have recourse to foreign producers in order to lower the demands of national labour; the pass-word would be given and would have the force of law everywhere.

I sincerely admire this organization, and I think that in skilful hands it will effect a rise in wages in a few years. It remains to be seen if working men would be sensibly better off, and this I deny.

Suppose that a well-conducted and well-sustained strike should have doubled the pay of the workmen belonging to a particular trade. The shoemakers, for example, would persist in selling for ten francs the labour they perform for five. What would be the consequence? The consumer, that is, everybody, would pay dearer for his shoes. Now the hatters, who do not walk about with bare feet, and who wish to balance their accounts, would feel the need of earning more, having more to pay. They would demand and obtain an increase of wages, and thus the rise in hats would immediately follow the rise in shoes. The tailors would be very simple if they suffered themselves to be fleeced without also fleecing their customers, and from needle to thread the rise in industrial wages would raise the prices of all manufacturers' products.

But the peasant is no stupider than the townsman. When he perceives that his clothing, his implements, and all the merchandise he consumes cost him more than formerly, he will no longer part with either his corn, his cattle, his wool, his wine, his flax, at the prices of the good old times. Since the time that city-traders sell their labour twice as dear, wherefore should he part with his own at a reduced rate? Reciprocity is a law which no one ignores. " I sell as I buy, and I make use of those who make use of me." The rise in agricultural products closely succeeds that in manufactured articles.

Public servants, that is, government clerks, soon perceive that they are dupes. " I work as much as ever, yet I receive the same salary; but the sum I obtain no longer enables me to live as comfortably, because all workers, excepting me, have doubled the price of their services. I do not refuse to pay the increase to the others, provided that I am better paid in return." Nothing can be more just: all the salaries are increased, and the two milliards in the Budget become four. Now, who is it that pays the Budget? Everybody.

And what will the worthy landlord say? What

will the capitalist say in presence of the universal rise in prices? Our taxes are doubled, we pay twice as much as formerly for the services of a peasant, of a workman, of a domestic ; is it not just and natural that our salary should be doubled, that is, the interest on our capital, the rent of our houses and lands?

In the long run, the shoemakers, who thought they had won a fine victory in doubling the rate of the service they sell, will perceive that at the same time they have doubled the price of all the services they purchase.

We have stated and proved that all men are at once producers and consumers. If we double our wages all round, each will gain cent. per cent. as producer and lose it as consumer, and nothing will be altered in the exchange of services. I err ; this general rise in prices will oblige us to turn over twice as much money, and, in consequence, to double our stock of the precious metals. The nation, which transacts all its exchanges with five milliards of gold, will see itself under the necessity of buying and holding ten, that is, of burdening itself with a frightful mass of unproductive capital.

CHAPTER XI.

CO-OPERATION.

IF strikes have still their fanatics, and even dangerous fanatics, in England, few partisans of them remain amongst us. For about two years the French appear to have turned against them without reason, out of fatigue, and chiefly owing to the attraction of a new and more seductive illusion. When the delegates of the English workmen propounded their great project of a general turn out, French workmen barely listened to them: "What matters it to us to raise the rate of wages when we are on the eve of suppressing wages and becoming our own masters?" A noble ambition, and a proud hope, testifying to an increase of virility in the minds of our working-men.

The honest man who dreams of a more independent position must not be discouraged, neither must he be ensnared. In societies on a democratic basis, where the vote of the majority confers power and dignity, the object of many is to flatter the illusions of the plebeians; all parties contend for the patronage of every popular idea, whether it be practicable or not. Whatever may be the result of experience, even when the end is an increase of poverty, the rogues who discounted the ambition of the poor retain the wages of their iniquities.

Co-operation, in the new sense given by democracy to this old word, means an association formed by workmen, destitute of capital, to purchase in common the necessaries of life without the intervention of the retail dealer ; or to produce in common, without having submitted to the master's orders ; or to lend their small savings to each other without having recourse to a banker. Societies for mutual consumption, production, and credit tend towards the same end, emancipation; by the same path, association.

The principle is laudable, and worthy of every encouragement; a man who will emancipate himself at his own risk is more of a man than those who tread the beaten path. The procedure common to all these co-operation societies (that is, association) is inspired by the best sentiments of human nature. It is to be wished, then, that the experiment of the three modes of co-operation should be made on a large scale, and should have all possible success.

But the duty of publicists, devoid of all personal ambition, is to inform the working-men, to illumine their path, and to warn them against the dangers of unbounded expectations.

Indeed, co-operative societies for articles of consumption meet a real want. The poor have always paid more than the rich, because they cannot buy their goods save in small quantities, at ninth or tenth hand. It is estimated that at Paris the articles of first necessity sold to the working-man undergo an increase of 38 to 40 per cent., that is, he pays seven francs for what a rich man would get for five. This added value is exorbitant, and yet logical. The worker has neither the time nor the means for buying his merchandise wholesale; he is not housed in a manner to be able to keep at home a stock of some extent; he must limit his daily purchases to his personal consumption. The 40 per cent. the worker gives in excess is not seized by parasites; it serves to pay the labour, the rent, and the risks, of a crowd of small producers, grocers, coal-merchants, water-carriers, sausage-makers, butchers, &c., who convey, preserve, and retail merchandise within reach of the small consumer. .

Clearly, the workman would be happier if he could get rid of this tax. The reduction of 40 per cent. in his purchases would be equivalent to a corresponding rise in his wages. Enable him to buy in small quantities at wholesale prices, and his day's work, for which he gets five francs, would fetch seven, without the master paying a single centime in addition, without the selling price of manufactured articles being raised a centime.

This is so striking a truth that several large manufacturers and some wealthy companies have given effect to it. The Orleans Railway Company has become a trader, and sells by retail for the profit of its 14,000 servants. It allows them to obtain by retail, at the wholesale price, food, wine, firing, linen, clothing, and generally, all the necessaries of life. In this way it increases the wages of its servants by 40 per cent. without opening its purse. However, it must not be supposed that this paternal part costs it nothing. The company lends the shops, it transports the articles gratis, it sets apart some of its servants to conduct the business, it bears the inevitable deterioration of merchandise, — in fine, it submits to a considerable outlay, with which, were not the cost compensated for in the well-being and attachment of 14,000 persons, it ought to debit itself.

The salt works of Dieuze, and other important establishments, supply their workmen with bread at cost price. At cost price, that is, under the actual cost, for they are not made to pay for firing, or for the storage of the material, for the rent of the buildings, nor for the labour expended.

Dollfus, Koechlin, Goldenberg, Monin, Japy, these great Alsatian manufacturers, who above all things are good men, have erected working-class dwellings which they dispose of at cost price. All this is intelligent, liberal, kind patronage; it is not co-operation.

A co-operative society for consumption would be one which purchased, for instance, ten thousand hectolitres of wine in the Hérault, at the price of ten francs the hectolitre, to distribute it in retail to three thousand members living in Paris, or one which ordered six thousand tons of coal from the pits of Anzin at ten francs the thousand kilogrammes, to dispose of them without profit to six thousand Parisian members.

To those who are acquainted with the prices of coals and wine charged by the Paris retail dealers, these two operations would appear admirable: "What! we should be able to get coal at 50 centimes the 50 kilogrammes! Genuine wine would not cost more than 10 centimes the litre!" Stay a moment. The cost of carriage and the duty must be added to the price of the wine, which in the case of cheap wines is 200 per cent. and upwards. A warehouse and spacious cellar must next be hired. Is that all? Unfortunately not. Working men have not the time to run to Neuilly or to la Rapée every time they require a sack of coal or a bottle of wine. Their time is worth money; it is of importance that articles in daily use should be obtainable close at hand, or at least may be had round the corner. It would thus be indispensable that the societies in question should have nearly as many branches in the city as there are coal-dealers and wine-merchants. The society would require to rent shops, pay wages to shopmen, to labourers, to superintendents, keep up an establishment far more onerous than that of the wine-merchant and his boy, the coal-dealer and his wife.

I do not say that the success of a large co-operative society is absolutely impossible, but at first sight I am sceptical about it. The English who, at first, were taken with this kind of operation, have communicated to us the list of their failures. Too often, nearly always, they have seen the workmen cheated by their agents, by the superintendents of the co-operative stores. They unanimously declare that the ruin or prosperity of such a society depends upon the choice of the manager, and that a competent, active, honest manager is a real white crow. The pioneer association in the co-operative movement gave the fol-

lowing advice to similar societies, in an address published in London in 1866 : 1. " Be sure that the
managers furnish good and trustworthy security. 2.
Make them an allowance of two per cent., at least,
for the depreciation of merchandise. 3. Insist upon
their books being correctly kept, audit them frequently, and balance them weekly. Everything
depends upon the morality of the managers. Success
rests entirely in their hands ; they cannot be selected
with too much caution and judgment. It is also of
vital importance to pay them well and give them
a share in the profits." The eminent economist
Cernuschi thus commented on the foregoing extract :
" Very exceptional men are required to act as
managers, find security, enter into contracts about
depreciation ; it is necessary to have very skilful
responsible agents and directors, to pay all these
persons, giving them, in addition, a share in the
profits, making the consumer bear all the losses.
When one is so well acquainted with the reasons
on the other side, can one advocate co-operative societies ? "

As for me, I do not advocate them, and yet I
would not set any one against them. Let whoever
will, try them, but with discretion. The official inquiry of 1866 has shown that in the opinion of nearly
all practical men, co-operative societies ought to

supply not their members only, but third parties also. They would not then suppress the actual middlemen except by replacing them, and after having killed the grocer, the wine-merchant, the coal-merchant, and so many other alleged parasites, they would step into their shoes. I do not perceive that third parties, that is, the non-associated consumers, would be the gainers by this substitution; nor am I even quite sure that the associated working men would realize large profits by engaging in trade. They have neither the aptitude, nor the funds, necessary for buying and selling, and they run the greater risk of losing their original stake, as they must transact business through the agency of a representative.

These considerations have determined several sections of intelligent working men to come to terms with traders instead of declaring war against them. At Mühlhausen, at Strassburg, and in several other manufacturing towns, the working man has given up the idea of establishing special stores. He enters on an amicable understanding with the established retail dealers, stipulating for a discount of five, six, and seven per cent. on all his purchases. He buys for ready money, pays for the articles of consumption at the regular price, and allows the product of his discounts to become capitalized in a common chest. This is not exactly co-operation, but it is well-organized saving. M. Emile Koechlin has calculated that these small discounts, added to a very trifling deposit, produce a minimum of 36 francs per head yearly, and that each member will amass 452 francs in ten years, 1190 francs in twenty years, and 2400 francs in thirty years, by the interest accumulated on his 36 francs per annum. Such is the unpretending combination which enables the working man to form a small capital without risking a centime, and without depriving himself of an iota.

Co-operative societies for mutual credit have been most successful in Germany, but it must not be hastily concluded that they have a brilliant future before them. The Germans have established more than a thousand, and it is estimated that these popular banks make advances to the extent of 500 millions yearly.

The mechanism of such an association is very simple. Half a hundred honest persons, all in business, small tradesmen, small masters, dwelling in the same parish, and acquainted with each other, subscribe to form a working capital. When one of them is pressed for money, he has recourse to the co-operative bank, which advances him 500 francs, if it possesses so much, in addition to 250, and even up to 500 francs, on the credit of the other partners. This is a real credit operation, for it is a token of confidence accorded by some honest men to a man whom they have reason to consider honest. The Credit Foncier does not give credit, it lends on mortgages, without considering the morality of the borrower; the Credit Mobilier does not give credit, any more than the State pawn-shop: they lend upon security. The true and only credit is a loan made on personal security, and the societies founded by Herr Schultze von Delitsch are the first credit institutions which have taken root in Europe.

A respectable and worthy Paris citizen, who was unacquainted with the name and work of Herr Schultze von Delitsch, originated among us the parent society of Mutual Credit. This good man's name is Engelmann, and his work dates from 1857. The first members began by subscribing one franc weekly: in 1866, that is, nine years afterwards, each of them had 543 francs in the common chest. The members of the parent society number forty-eight, scattered over the different parts of Paris; they are recruited in a large number of industries, for if they were all in the same line of business, the slightest crisis would have destroyed them at a stroke. This handful of bold men, with limited means, has been able to advance 252,223 francs in eight years. The sum-total of their losses during these eight years amounted to five francs.

This is admirable, and I should have sincerely regretted if this parent society had been without offspring. It has given birth to sixty or seventy other associations, each of which numbers from twenty-five to fifty members.

It is to be hoped that mutual credit will not halt in so fine a path, and that associations of the same kind will be multiplied in Paris and in the provinces. But mutual credit is absolutely incapable of solving the working man's problem, and advancing the social reform which rich and poor alike long to witness.

The object of the combination of M. Engelmann and of Herr Schultze von Delitsch is to assure small masters against all the accidents which might throw them back into the working-class gulf; it is gradually making its way among the higher bourgeoisie, which is very praiseworthy and very gratifying, but it is unfitted for transforming the working man, the man who has nothing, into a small capitalist. The members of a society of mutual credit are all men in business, they present something tangible, they offer guarantees to their partners, they are few enough in number to know and to rate each other at their proper value. Lowly though their lot is, these men would appear to you a genuine aristocracy, if you compared them with pure working men, with the legion of men without capital, without furniture,

without fixed place of abode, whom the smallest
accident sends from one furnished room to another,
from one district to another, from one workshop to
another; too happy if the chances of industry do not
rudely throw them into the streets. Who is there that
would lend them the smallest sum wherewith to set
up for themselves? Who knows anything about
them, unless it be their comrades, as poor as themselves? A hundred small capitals might be joined
together, and converted into large sums; the association of a hundred distresses would but form a
gigantic distress.

The working man abuses his position so slightly
as not even to attempt to borrow from the small
bourgeois; he rather lends him his savings. M.
Engelmann said in his evidence at the inquiry into
co-operative societies, "As for working men, who
hardly ever borrow, our society is for them a sort of
savings'-bank. I am almost certain that even if one
should select a thousand picked workmen out of all the
French manufactories, and offer them a thousand
francs per head at five per cent. in order that each
might set up on his own account, nearly all of them
would resist the allurements of capital."

The time has gone by when the first-class workman dreamed of setting up on his own account as
artificer or small master. A revolution has taken

place in the opinion of the workshops; one has begun to understand that the existence of small shops is menaced by manufacturers; one participates in a war in which large battalions, that is, large capital, are assured of victory. One also feels (for fair-mindedness is shown) that an excellent workman in one branch would make a bad general workman. The division of labour develops certain phases of talent to the detriment of all the others. In order to be a workman of exceptional character, and to earn large wages, it is necessary to be able to do this thing or that thing well; a good artizan must know how to do everything, or at least a little of everything; he must be more finished a workman than the leading men in any manufacture. Finally, the whole truth must be told: the cream of the working class aspire to do things on a large scale, to turn over millions of money, and to give work to thousands of hands. The superior members of the wages class see or consider that they are on the eve of an economic movement comparable to the great rising of the volunteers in 1792, and each hopes that he has got his marshal's baton in his pocket.

M. Batbie, a very distinguished economist, said, during the inquiry in 1866: "Of the three forms of co-operative societies, I consider that formed for purposes of production the most difficult to consti-

tute, and yet it is the one most in favour with working men. The co-operative producing societies are
the most popular, and those who wish to please the
working man do not hesitate to recommend them."
As for us who desire to enlighten, and not to please
them, we do not dread discussion.

Let it be frankly admitted that co-operative producing societies are organized against the masters.
Many working men believe themselves mulcted by
their master; they think that wages, according to
the bold phrase of M. Limousin, constitute so much
paid to account on the product of labour, and when
they are told that wages are fixed rates, beyond
which no one owes anything, they call out that they
are robbed.

This opinion was so deeply rooted twenty years
ago, that the first act of the working men, after the
downfall of King Louis Philippe, was to organize
themselves in fraternal societies in which everybody
was the master. Whatever their prejudices against
infamous capital, they understood it would have been
madness to begin their enterprises without it. The
Provisional Government came to their aid with a
loan of three millions. Three hundred producing
societies were formed; they have paid nothing back,
and two hundred and eighty-four out of the three
hundred have become defunct. It must be said that

politics, after smiling upon their birth, were accomplices in their death.

In my opinion, it is sufficient that sixteen of them
should survive and prosper to a certain extent, in order not to feel discouraged about new attempts at
co-operation. But it would be deceiving the working men to tell them, " The State will lend you
money again." They must trust to themselves alone,
and must not expect any capital save that derived
from their personal saving.

Now, there are industries which must not be undertaken without plenty of money. Everybody knows
that at the present day the most perfect machinery
gives the best results at the most favourable rate ;
that an inadequately-arranged manufactory must
supply goods at a higher price than a manufactory
of the first-class, and that the consumer will always prefer the cheapest merchandise if the quality
be equally good. It is impossible, then, with a
small capital, that is, wretched machinery, to maintain competition with millions equipped for the fray.
For example, a spinning-mill worth 100,000, or even
300,000 francs, is doomed to die before its birth.

It must be admitted, then, above all, that co-
operative producing societies have no call to embark
in industries which are carried on by means of
capital.

Some flatterers have told the working class : " You have but to will it, in order to establish a manufactory requiring two millions and a half. A hundred thousand working men would subscribe for a year at the rate of 50 centimes weekly. By the 31st of December they would have collected the sum of 2,600,000 francs." Nothing can be more true. But do you think that machinery costing 2,600,000 francs could give employment to 100,000 pairs of arms ? It would not require 500. Out of the 100,000 members who expect to become masters, there would thus be 95,000 who would have failed in their expectation. Who would be the privileged ones ? Lots might be drawn. This would be a fairer game than the infamous 25 centimes lotteries, yet I should not take upon myself to recommend it to any one.

The working men who dream of emancipating themselves by means of co-operative production would do well to select industries in which manual labour is more required than capital. They should carefully avoid those where capital furnishes ninety-five parts out of a hundred and manual labour five, like upholstering, for instance. They should give the preference to those where man's labour adds a considerable value to materials of little worth.

In the inquiry about co-operative societies, M.

Émile Laurent has told the history of an association which began with a capital of two francs : " With this capital a log of wood was bought, and it was sold for seven or eight francs; with this sum several logs were bought. This society is at present one of the largest in Paris for the manufacture of lasts." Suppose for a moment that the journeyman diamond-cutters were to form a co-operative society. Do you think they would arrive at a like result in starting with a capital of two francs ?

Working spectacle-makers produce 60 francs' worth of work out of 15 francs' worth of raw materials. In their case manual labour adds 75 per cent. to the value of the product. Thus they were in an excellent condition for forming themselves into a co-operative society; hence they have been entirely successful. But, after having started without capital (they were in debt to the extent of 650 francs in 1849), they found out the importance of summoning money to their help. Listen to the evidence of M. Delabre : " The common contribution was fixed at 300 francs, but we ascertained that it was insufficient. New members joined, and the contribution was raised to 1000, then to 5000 and 10,000 francs; we even think of raising it to 1,500,000 francs. This year (1866) we have done business to the extent of

600,000 francs." They do business to the extent of
600,000 francs, but their paid-up capital is 300,000
francs (evidence of M. Muneaux).

The trade of chair-turners, like that of last-
makers and spectacle-makers, adds a considerable
extra value to the raw materials. A co-operative
society founded by them in 1848, has attracted seven
hundred members, who do business to the extent of
200,000 francs upon a capital of 60,000 francs. Out
of the seven hundred members, only eleven remained
in 1866, and the evidence of M. Surugue, which is
very interesting, does not fully account for this falling off. I am tempted to think that individualism
(excuse the word) will frequently draw away French
workmen from the most lucrative association.

The advocates of production in common, bring
forward in opposition to all critiques the really
splendid success of the co-operative society of masons.
The society of masons of Paris, like the free pioneers
of Rochdale, represents the ideal of triumphant co-
operation. I allow that it is difficult not to admire the
success of the masons' co-operative society. Eighty
pairs of arms, united in severe labour, succeed by their
own powers in terminating gigantic works like the
new Orleans railway station ; this is truly a miracle of
human energy. But these arms are not a blind force ;
they are disciplined, subjected to the controlling

direction of two or three able men. Read the evidence of M. Cohadon, manager of this society, and you will think you are hearing the voice of a master who is extremely well instructed and very distinguished in every way. If the masons of the Rue St Victoire have constituted themselves a republic, they have been careful to elect first-class presidents.

Although building operations are those in which manual labour has more value than the raw material, the society of working masons has taken care not to break with capital. It formed a working capital of 300,000 francs; the share of certain members is 2000 francs and even 10,000 francs, and as the united workers could not raise the 300,000 francs by means of subscriptions, they did not hesitate to have recourse to the capital of the bourgeois. In this prosperous society "Capital has its function alongside of labour, and it then divides the profits with the manual labourer." It is M. Cohadon who says this: a master could not express himself better. In the division of profits, " 60 per cent. are apportioned to labour, 40 per cent. to capital." Is not this a perfectly equitable proportion?

The working men receive a fixed wage, which is regulated by the quantity and quality of their labour; afterwards they have a share in the profits, just as they will have to divide the losses in the event of misfortune.

This co-operative society will appear the less revolutionary to you the more closely you study it. It sanctions the rights of capital, it admits wages, it recompenses the workers in proportion to their services, and pays the manager more than the manual labourer, without regarding him as a parasite. It is an eighty-headed master, who argues and defends his interests like all other masters. This co-operative society gives employment to hundreds of workmen, and pays them a fixed, unvarying, final wage, one which is in no respect so much on account of the produce of labour. Only, these workers bear the flattering name of auxiliaries. Nothing can be in greater contradiction to the principles of theoretic co-operation. But listen to M. Cohadon, who is a man with a practical mind : " This is why it is impossible not to employ auxiliaries ; customers cannot be turned away when they offer employment, otherwise it would be lost. In principle, an association ought only to make its members work, but this is materially impossible in practice. It is equally impossible to promise the auxiliaries a share in the profits. Firstly, is one certain of always making profits ? And if there are losses, ought or could the auxiliaries bear their proportion ? And, then, is it possible to grant the auxiliaries a right of interference in the society's affairs? How shall we settle their quota? How shall we justify their good faith? . . . It is not admissible that those who do not share in the losses should share in the profits."

I am not sorry to hear a sensible workman speak in this fashion, and turn against the receivers of wages the eternal arguments of the masters. There is not any head of a manufactory who has not held this language twenty times in refutation of the demands of his workmen. If the workman himself, as soon as he becomes a fractional master, adopts the ideas of our good old social economy, it is because we are in the right. I am pleased to register this homage rendered by co-operation to the fundamental principle of the master's position.

M. Blaise (of the Vosges), who is a very able economist, expressed himself as follows on this head, before a commission of inquiry: "From the legal point of view the operations of the producing societies are identical with those of the masters; from the moral point of view, they proceed in almost the same manner. Like them, they employ wage-receivers, called auxiliaries, do not pay them more and do not ensure them constant employment; these workmen even complain about being treated worse than by their ordinary masters. These societies, when their

13

members possess the rare technical and commanding business qualities which ensure success, profit their founders, or those who are afterwards admitted; but they merely represent more masters, and though they may be still greatly increased in number, yet as they can never include more than a fraction of the working class, they are not bound to exercise a serious influence on the economic condition of the masses."

I do not go quite so far, but I fear that, in the producing societies, many will be called and few chosen.

M. Chabaud, president of the working class delegates at the universal exhibition of 1862, and founder of several co-operative societies, is of opinion that "the producing societies might end indeed by abolishing the masters, but that will not happen for a long time to come." I believe this the more willingly because M. Chabaud has told us himself: "In order that a society should succeed, it must have at its head a man of superior intelligence, of unimpeachable honesty, and of unequalled abnegation. It is often difficult to meet with such a man." Assuredly, and all of that stamp who are met with ought to be taken from the workshop and made into deputies, prefects, senators, ambassadors, and ministers.

CHAPTER XII.

INTELLIGENT reader, you must understand that if I held in my hand the solution of the problem of poverty, I should not have kept you waiting for it till the last chapter of my book.

The malady is as old as the world; all those who have conscientiously studied it (and I am one of them) affirm that the cure will be long and difficult. It is rendering some service to the patient to forewarn him against the quacks who promise to cure him in a week. It is also something to re-establish the true remedies, which are well known, but are far too little employed in these days.

All men wish to possess something; this ambition is not merely natural, but praiseworthy. "In order to possess something, one must either inherit it, or work for it, or win a prize in a lottery" (Cernuschi). I put aside the lottery, which is but an impudent trading on human imbecility, and I say that those who have not the good fortune to inherit anything, ought not to expect anything save from their own exertions and their personal savings. All the theories which promise them property, otherwise gotten, are snares. To consume daily a little less than we produce is the only source of capital, whether small or great.

I allow that the act of piling sou upon sou is not very attractive in itself. Yet the effect of this practice is certain to render toil more pleasing and less hard. Those who exist from day to day, absorbing all their wages as they earn them, have no encouragement to labour here below. Their life is objectless; the past, the present, the future resemble each other; they feel that in twenty years they will be no farther advanced than to day. This being so, why exert themselves?

From the time that the working man has begun the small hoard which must either emancipate him from labour or else assure the repose of his old age, the face of everything is changed. He sees his end; he walks with confidence, he gladly admits that each step brings him nearer to it. The monotony of his occupations disappear from his eyes, because each day leads to a personal change in himself; he feels himself become another man in proportion as he grows richer. He who labours without acquiring anything does not know why he labours; he who sees his savings increase says to himself every morning with redoubled courage, "I labour for my own behoof." .

This provident selfishness is a far more powerful spring than the necessity of earning one's daily bread. The worker who thinks about the future is a different fellow from the mercenary resigned to perpetual beggary, who limits his wants to spare his efforts, and arrives at consuming the smallest possible quantity by fatiguing himself to the smallest possible extent.

But the strongest of workers is he who saves for the sake of his children. Marry; the expenses of house-keeping are not to be compared to its gains. All privations become pleasures, from the moment that one stints oneself for those one loves.

Get instruction if you can; I have stated that the labour of the instructed man is worth more than that of the illiterate. If you are past the age for learning, do not fail to send your children to school, in order that they may one day become happier and . more useful than yourself. Seek by every means to enlighten yourself as to the questions of social economy, were it merely to put yourself on your guard against the devices of impostors.

You knew all that, did you not? Yet each time that you wished to make a forward step you have been stopped by some obstacle. In the first place, it was the dearness of living which rendered it difficult to economize. Next, the trifling sum you put aside brought you in but the small interest of three and a half per cent., at the Savings' Bank. At this rate, much time is required to increase your small capital. And no one is certain of living long enough to turn it into a good round sum! Even when one succeeds in realizing a thousand or two thousand francs, how is one to set up on one's own account with so little? Artizans and shop-keepers are subject to the commercial law, which is severe; their customers are subject to the civil law, which is infinitely more gentle. The working man who founds a firm without large capital buys raw material at sixty or ninety days. If he do not pay for them punctually he is declared bankrupt, arrested, ruined, and dishonoured; such is the law of trade. His customers, richer than himself, pay him when they think fit, when nothing is more pressing, at the end of one year, two years, and sometimes later still. Such is the general custom, encouraged by the delays and facilities of the civil law. The consequence is that a worthy man may legally fall into difficulties, although he is owed more than he owes;

in a single day he loses the savings of twenty years.

It is easy to tell working men, Study social economy. Where are the cheap books and pamphlets written in their language, and fitted to instruct them? They are advised to send their children to school; they answer, We should like nothing better, but we have not all got the means of paying for this humble primary instruction.

I do not dispute the value of these arguments, but I consider that they admit of replies. The working men have got the suffrage in their own right hands; they do not know how best to dispose of it in their interests. They suffer themselves to be enrolled in one party to-day, in another to-morrow; when will they begin a peaceful campaign on behalf of their wives and their children? When will they sketch the programme of reasonable reforms, of which they stand in need, to better their condition?

There is no question about raising the standard of a new opposition. We live under a government which has always declared and shown itself neutral in economical matters; schemes of social amelioration have adherents disseminated among all parties, on the right and the left of the Assemblies.

If the members of the wages-class would come to an understanding they would form the necessary majority at all elections. The constitution forbids them sending representatives pledged to take a line, but it does not prohibit them from expressing in some newspapers what they expect from their representatives.

Do they desire cheap food ? Then let them elect representatives who are the friends of Free Trade ? Do they wish to drink genuine wine at a low price ? Then let them support the revision of the octroi tariffs, let them propose the sale of wines by public auction and the imposition of an *ad valorem* duty. Were this duty as much as cent. per cent., the Parisian workman would drink at home an agreeable and generous wine at 30 centimes the litre. Do they wish their children to go to school ? Let them elect representatives who approve of gratuitous instruction. Are they anxious for enlightenment on all points of social economy ? Let them cause a motion to be made for the abolition of the tax on instructive pamphlets. It is by means of the penny paper that practical notions have entered the minds of the English working men, and the penny paper can never be produced if it must bear an eight centime stamp.

Working men complain, and rightly too, of never getting more than three and a half per cent. interest from the Savings' Bank. They say, " Why is it that when we borrow a milliard as citizens, members of

the great French Community, we should pay five, or
at least four and a half, per cent. interest, and when
we lend our own savings we cannot get four per cent.?"
My friends, look after your pockets. Elect representatives who will advocate your interests. The Savings'
Bank can pay four and a half per cent. without
injury to any one. A rise of one per cent. in the
interest it pays would soon double its deposits (which
amount to 528 millions), that is, would induce increased saving, and render a multitude of citizens
more prudent. The matter would be a good one for
the depositors, better still for the nation. Rich and
poor, we are all interested in extending the class of
small capitalists.

And in order that the small capitalists should be
able to set up for themselves without too many becoming bankrupts, use your electoral rights as working men. Redouble your personality, so that the
citizen may help the private individual. Call for a
law which should harmonize the Civil Code with the
Commercial Code. Cause it to be decided in principle that " All goods and services shall bear
six per cent. interest from the day succeeding their
delivery." This simple clause would soon habituate
customers in easy circumstances to pay their providers
and workmen in cash; nothing more is needed to
spare small capitalists, whether united or isolated,

many miscarriages.   The innovation I here recommend is not unknown in England.

Finally, if you are not certain about living long enough to become capitalists yourselves, make such arrangements as will enable you to leave an offspring of bourgeois by assuring your life for your children's profit.   City and country working men have known and supported for some time two prudential societies, which are—1. The Society of Mutual Assistance against the sad incapacities which are the consequence of sickness, of want of employment.   2. Assurance against the privations which are the consequence of weakness, of old age.

A friendly society is a lottery in an inverted fashion, where the bad members win.   Some hundreds of workers club together a trifling portion of their savings.   The capital thus created belongs, in virtue of an equitable and moral arrangement, to those of the members who are marked out by misfortune.   It is an excellent institution, upon which capitalists everywhere bestow an active and disinterested support.   Rich or well-to-do citizens who join a society of this kind, as honorary members, do not perform an act of individual benevolence, but of social foresight.   We are all interested in helping those of our honest and brave fellow-citizens who begin by helping themselves.

The Bank of Annuities for old age enables the

working man to secure bread for his last days by a trifling contribution from his wages.

A new institution, the Assurance against Accidents, invites workers of all classes to guard against the sudden strokes which lead to permanent unfitness for work. The working man, by a payment of eight, five, and three francs at will, may protect himself for a whole year. Should he be accidentally smitten with a total incapacity for work, the State, his assurer, allows him for life a sum of 5120 francs, or 3200 francs, or 1920 francs, according to the amount of his contribution. This capital produces an income naturrally proportioned to the age of the person assured, but which cannot be less than 200 francs for contributions of five francs, and 150 francs for contributions of three francs.

If the accident be of a nature to cause permanent incapacity for your professional labours, without wholly hindering you from embarking in another pursuit, the figure of the sum paid is reduced to one-half. In case of the death of the person assured, his widow, his children who are minors, or his aged parents, will receive, in the form of assistance, two annuities of the pension to which they would have been entitled.

You perceive at first sight that the small payments of eight, five, and three francs are not proportioned to the advantages reaped by the person assured. It was necessary that society, in other words, the State, should come to the help of the working men by doubling the yield of their savings. Each time a working man performs an act of foresight by paying in a sum of five francs, the mass of French citizens performs an act of patronage by giving a corresponding sum. The persons assured will receive at least the double of what would be due to them without this friendly intervention. It is not alms which are bestowed, but brotherly encouragement which is given, in the common interest of rich and poor. This institution will have the result of assuaging much distress, but it will not create a single capitalist. It is the Life Assurance Company which enables you to leave something to your heirs without submitting to too great privations.

Among the working men living from hand to mouth, there is perhaps not one who has failed frequently to say, "If I had but a small capital! two or three thousand francs, or even a single thousand-franc note, I should be another man, freer, stronger, more useful to others and to myself."

The law replies to the poor day labourer who laments thus, "My friend, your father has done nothing for you, you may do something for your children. Arrange so as to save 17 francs 70 centimes in a year, if you are thirty; 23 francs 50, rather less than two sous daily, if you have reached forty. If you have arrived at the age of fifty without learning about the admirable resources of assurance, it will cost you more, but not much. The trifling sacrifice of two sous a day will enable you to bequeath to your son a capital of one thousand francs, payable on the day after your death." Thus the working man of thirty, if he give a sou daily, the working man of forty if he give a sou and a half, the working man of fifty if he give ten centimes, provides for a capital of a thousand francs being paid to his heirs, whatever be the period of his death. I err. The law, in order to save those who are assured from the cost and annoyance of medical inspection, and to prevent at the same time a person assuring when at the last gasp, ordains that every assurance contracted less than two years prior to the death of the person assured is void. His assigns will have restored to them the sum deposited, with interest at four per cent. But on the expiry of two years and a day, if the person assured should die, his family acquires the thousand francs. A man of fifty-three who should be struck down in the third year of the contract would have paid 106 francs 50 centimes only, and would leave one thousand francs to his children. A young married man who assures at twenty and dies at twenty-three, will leave the thousand francs to his widow; he will only have paid in 40 francs 90 centimes on three occasions.

The State has not desired to compete with the companies which assure for large amounts; its aim being to enable the working man to participate in the benefits of a new discovery. This is why the sum which can be assured per head is limited to 3000 francs.

In order to leave 3000 francs to his heirs, a person who assures at seventeen undertakes to save 40 francs 20 centimes yearly, or about 11 centimes a day; a man who assures at thirty will deposit 53 francs 10 centimes yearly, or a little more than a franc weekly. You see that a good, and even a mediocre, workman has no need to bleed himself in order to breed capitalists.

But assurance is lightest chiefly to those who commence in their youth. The annual premium is at a minimum for those whose chances of paying longest are the greatest; the premium rises in proportion as your probable limit of life becomes shorter. The man of sixty who desired to leave 3000 francs to his son or grandson would have to deposit 45 centimes a day. In reality, the capital would not cost him more than it would cost the young man of seventeen who undertook to pay 11 centimes during a long life;

but the deduction of 11 centimes from an average wage is not appreciable, whilst the diminution of 45 centimes from even a high wage would appear trying. Then assure without delay. In that, as in all good things, the sooner the better.

Should this novelty find the favour with the public which it deserves, the problem of the working class, which recently seemed insoluble, will have been solved in principle now, and in fact before thirty years elapse.

But shall the honest and provident working men who deprive themselves of comforts, and deny themselves certain enjoyments, in the interest of the next generation, reap no fruits from such splendid devotion? Is it fair that the present should be absolutely sacrificed for the future? Certainly not.

The man who has taken care to assure himself for 3000 francs becomes, for that reason alone, a negociable value at the end of a few years. He is worth more in the market than the pure and simple worker. Prior to assuring, he would have had difficulty in finding a neighbour generous enough to advance him 100 francs at five per cent. It is folly to confide the smallest capital to a man whose whole possession is his arms and who may die any day. But if my late or premature decease legally opens up a succession to 3000 francs, if the law authorize me to alienate by deed the half of that amount, my personal credit, that is, the esteem I have been able to inspire, is doubled by a real guaranty. The lender knows that I shall repay him myself, if I live, and that in case of accident my death will repay him. One may then, without risk, place a small capital at my service; I can set up for myself and become a bourgeois myself, from having had the generous notion of begetting bourgeois.

THE END.

www.ingramcontent.com/pod-product-compliance
Lightning Source LLC
Chambersburg PA
CBHW031406270326
41929CB00010BA/1350